Be Strong & Be Brave...
for the Lord your God is with you.
Deuteronomy 31:6

By
Kristie Kerr & Paula Yarnes
with
Jeff Kerr & Aaron Broberg

Copyright 2015 Kristie Kerr and Paula Yarnes. All Rights Reserved.

No part of this book may be reproduced, transmitted, or utilized in any form or by any means, graphic, electronic or mechanical, including photocopying, recording, taping, or by any information storage or retrieval, without the permission in writing from the publisher.

Unless otherwise indicated, all Scripture quotations are taken from the Holy Bible, New Living Translation, copyright ©1996, 2004, 2007 by Tyndale House Foundation. Used by permission of Tyndale House Publishers, Inc., Carol Stream, Illinois 60188. All rights reserved.

THE HOLY BIBLE, NEW INTERNATIONAL VERSION®, NIV® Copyright © 1973, 1978, 1984, 2011 by Biblica, Inc.™ Used by permission. All rights reserved worldwide.

Scripture taken from The Message. Copyright ©1993, 1994, 1995, 1996, 2000, 2001, 2002. Used by permission of NavPress Publishing Group.

Scripture taken from the Contemporary English Version ©1991, 1992, 1995 by American Bible Society, Used by Permission.

Scripture taken from the Common English Bible P.O. Box 801 201 Eighth Avenue South Nashville, TN 37202-0801

Scripture taken from the International Standard Version Release 2.1. Copyright ©1996–2012 the ISV Foundation. All rights reserved internationally.

Scripture taken from the Holy Bible, NEW INTERNATIONAL READER'S VERSION®. Copyright © 1996, 1998 Biblica. All rights reserved throughout the world. Used by permission of Biblica.

Scripture quotations taken from the 21st Century King James Version®, copyright © 1994. Used by permission of Deuel Enterprises, Inc., Gary, SD 57237. All rights reserved.

ISBN: 978-0-9970676-3-7

Printed in the United States of America

1st Printing

CONTENTS

We Need Each Other............ 1-20
- Lesson 2
- Doodle Page 10
- Activity Sheet 11
- Bazooka Breakdown 15
- Bazooka Project................ 19

Friendship 21-39
- Lesson 22
- Doodle Page 28
- Activity Sheet 29
- Bazooka Breakdown 34
- Bazooka Project............... 38

My Family 41-59
- Lesson 42
- Doodle Page 48
- Activity Sheet 49
- Bazooka Breakdown 52
- Bazooka Project............... 59

Elders 61-77
- Lesson 62
- Doodle Page 70
- Activity Sheet 71
- Bazooka Breakdown 74
- Bazooka Project............... 76

Things Change 79-94
- Lesson 80
- Doodle Page 88
- Activity Sheet 89
- Bazooka Breakdown 91
- Bazooka Project................94

Watch Your Words............... 95-111
- Lesson 96
- Doodle Page 102
- Activity Sheet 103
- Bazooka Breakdown 108
- Bazooka Project 111

Attention 113-133
- Lesson 114
- Doodle Page 120
- Activity Sheet 122
- Bazooka Breakdown 127
- Bazooka Project 131

Mean People 135-153
- Lesson 136
- Doodle Page 142
- Activity Sheet 144
- Bazooka Breakdown 149
- Bazooka Project 152

Do The Right Thing.......... 155-171
- Lesson 156
- Doodle Page 162
- Activity Sheet 163
- Bazooka Breakdown 168
- Bazooka Project 171

DEDICATION

Dedicated to the boys who inspire us:

To Charlie whose tender heart and quiet spirit
remind us that **STRENGTH ISN'T ALWAYS LOUD**.

To Hunter who is **TENACIOUS AND KIND**...
and came up with the name Bazooka Boys.

To Chase who **LOVES UNCONDITIONALLY**.

To Reed who lit his homework on fire...
and then became an **HONOR STUDENT**.

To Jacob, the boy with the sensitive heart,
that captures people with his **LOVE FOR JUSTICE AND ALL THINGS SILLY**.

To Levi whose **DETERMINATION COULD DEMOLISH MOUNTAINS**
& smile could melt away the debris

To Zach who is a **TRUSTWORTHY, CONFIDENT, KIND-HEARTED** young man,
and NEVER forgets to kiss his mom goodnight!

To Li who is **KIND AND LOVING** and **ALWAYS** follows the rules!

To Stewart. The **TWINKLE IN YOUR EYE** and the tenderness in your heart
remind us that God really does make dreams come true.

You amaze us.
Go change the world.

WE NEED EACH OTHER

WHAT'S THE POINT?
GOD CREATED US TO SHARE OUR LIVES WITH OTHER PEOPLE.

THEME VERSE:

Treat people in the same way that you want them to treat you.
Luke 6:31 (CEB)

RELATED BIBLE PASSAGE:

God gives Adam a companion
Genesis 2

It's not very much fun being by yourself. Can you imagine what it would be like if you didn't have any friends or family? I don't think that would be very much fun at all!

God made us with a desire for relationships. There's something inside of us that needs to have other people in our lives.

The Bible tells us that God created everything—the entire universe and everything in it was created by Him! But that wasn't His greatest creation. Oh no—the greatest thing God made was **US**! The Bible tells us the first person God created was a man named Adam. He was the very first person on the earth. Genesis 2:7 says, *"Then the Lord God formed the man from the dust of the ground. He breathed the breath of life into the man's nostrils, and the man became a living person."*

Adam lived in the beautiful Garden of Eden. It had everything He could have ever wanted inside of it. But one thing was missing: someone Adam could share his life with. In Genesis 2:18, God said, *"It is not good for the man to be alone."* God knew we needed other people in our lives to talk to, encourage and support, and be there for.

So God made Eve, the very first woman. Not only was she Adam's wife, she was Adam's friend. The Bible calls her Adam's helper or companion. A companion is someone who is by your side as you go on a journey. God gave Adam a companion to walk with him through the journey of life. No matter what was going to happen in Adam's life, he had someone who would be alongside him!

Isn't that cool? Out of all the cool things God gives us (and He gives us **LOTS** of really cool things) friendship and companionship are His best ideas! God doesn't make us go through

life all by ourselves. He gives us family and friends, pastors and teachers, neighbors and classmates to share our lives with us.

I am so thankful for all the relationships God has given me. I'm thankful for my mom and dad, who have loved me and taken good care of me. I'm thankful for the friends God has given me who make me laugh and do crazy things with me. I'm thankful for teachers who have taught me how to do things and helped me learn all kinds of important stuff. (Yes, even the math teachers! Even though I **REALLY** hated math class . . .)

God doesn't want us to go through life by ourselves. He **KNOWS** it's not good for us to be alone, so He gives us people to share our lives with. Sometimes it can feel like you're all alone, but the truth is that God has provided **LOTS** of people who care about you, love you, and want to be your companion as you grow and learn about life.

BAZOOKA BOYS BONUS

Take a minute to think of three people who are **COMPANIONS** in your life. Maybe it's your Mom and Dad? Maybe a special friend? Maybe your teacher or pastor? God has blessed you with lots of people who care about you!

God blesses us by giving us people in our lives. They are a gift to us. And just like any gift we're given, we need to appreciate them and take care of them. We need to be thankful for the friends and family God has given us and make sure we work really hard at being a good friend, son, student, classmate, and family member.

But let's be really honest. Our relationships are one of our greatest blessings, but they can also be one of our biggest problems! We can have fights with our friends. Our brothers can pick on us. We can get frustrated with our parents. Our teachers can make us mad. And our neighbors can hurt our feelings.

God knows how important your relationships are to you, and He wants to help you with them! The Bible is full of instructions to help us work out all the problems in our relationships. There are things God tells us to do to be a good friend. He shows us what kind of attitude we should have toward our parents. He helps us by showing us how to treat people who aren't kind and loving to us. God wants to help you with your relationships!

No matter what kind of questions you have about your relationships, God has the answers. He promises to help you with **ALL** the relationships in your life because He knows how important they are.

In the next few weeks and months, we're going to take a look at all the relationships in our lives. We're going to check out what the Bible has to say about being a good friend. We're going to learn how to treat people and how to behave in order to take really, really good care of all the relationships God has given us.

God gives us really specific ideas for taking care of our relationships, but there's one verse in the Bible that will be our theme throughout the next few weeks. It's a magic secret weapon that you can use in **ANY** relationship, at **ANY** time, in **ANY** place—no matter what the situation may be. Are you ready? Do you want to hear God's magic, super-secret weapon for having good relationships?

Okay…here it is. Are you **SURE** you're ready? It's a **REALLY** big deal. Okay . . . I think you're ready now:

"Treat people in the same way that you want them to treat you."—Luke 6:31 (CEB)

It seems pretty simple, right? Treat other people the way **YOU** want to be treated. Any time you're faced with a situation and you wonder what you should say or do, all you have to do is ask yourself the question, "How would I want someone to treat **ME** if I was in the same situation?" and you'll have your answer.

We should treat people the way we want to be treated. If you're wondering if you should say something, ask yourself how you would feel if someone said

that exact same thing about **YOU**. If you're wondering if you should do something, ask yourself how **YOU** would feel if someone did the same thing to you.

God wants you to treat other people the way you want to be treated. When you do this, your relationships will grow stronger. And strong relationships are super important because they're such a valuable part of our lives.

Here are three reasons your relationships are so important!

 1. YOUR RELATIONSHIPS HELP YOU GROW.

Josh never really felt like he was good at anything. While his friends were getting better at baseball and playing the drums, Josh simply watched from the sidelines. He really wanted to be good at something, but he just couldn't seem to find the thing he **LOVED** to do.

But when he started third grade, he had a new teacher named Mrs. Schneider. Mrs. Schneider seemed to see something in Josh that he had never seen in himself. She noticed that Josh really enjoyed the times in class where they got to work on computers. So one day, she asked Josh to create a special presentation for the class.

Josh found himself super nervous about the project, but super excited, too. The more he worked on the project, the more he realized how much he really enjoyed creating things on the computer. It came really easy to him, and he found himself working for hours without even noticing.

When Josh grew up, he got a job working with computers! He loves his work and is really, really good at it. There are many times when he thinks about Mrs. Schneider and how she helped him discover his love of computers. He often wonders if he would be doing what he's doing without the encouragement and support she gave him in third grade.

God will bring people into your life that will help you grow. He'll use them to show you new things, inspire you to try something different, and even help you find your gifts and talents. You'll have friends who will cheer you on as you discover the things you are good at. You'll have family members who will help you see something in yourself that you may have never seen on your own. God uses other people to help us grow in all kinds of areas of our lives!

The second reason relationships are so important is:

2. YOUR RELATIONSHIPS HELP YOU RUB OFF THE ROUGH EDGES.

Caleb had developed a bad habit. When other people were trying to tell him a story, he would interrupt them. He wasn't trying to be rude, he would just think of what he wanted to say and blurt it out without thinking.

One day, his very best friend in the whole wide world, Nick, was telling him something when he once again jumped in and interrupted. Nick took a deep breath and gently stopped him and said, "Caleb, I was telling you a story and you interrupted me. You are my best friend, but it really bugs me when you do that."

At first, Caleb was mad! "I don't do that," he thought to himself. But then he realized that Nick was right …he really hadn't been listening and had rudely interrupted his friend. He had a decision to make. He could get upset at Nick and storm off, or he could admit that he had a bad habit and start listening to his friend.

"I'm sorry," Caleb said. "I shouldn't have interrupted you. Please finish your story."

Bazooka Boys ★ Relationships

"WOUNDS FROM A SINCERE FRIEND ARE BETTER THAN MANY KISSES FROM AN ENEMY."
—PROVERBS 27:6

We **ALL** have things we need to work on in our lives. **NONE** of us are perfect, and there are always areas of our lives where we can get rid of some stuff that isn't the best.

MANY times, God will use the other people in our lives to help us see things we need to work on. And even though it can be hard to take sometimes, knowing that our friends love us and want to help us makes all the difference. Proverbs 27:6 tells us, *"Wounds from a sincere friend are better than many kisses from an enemy."* What that means is, even though it's never fun to hear things that we're doing wrong, we can trust that our friends want to help us. We can trust that when they tell us something, they're doing it out of love because they want the best for us.

A good friend will help you stop a bad habit. Your mom and dad can help you get over a behavior that isn't good so you don't hurt other people with your actions. A teacher can show you how to overcome a problem and figure out a new way to do things.

Have you ever used sandpaper before? When you're working with wood, you rub sandpaper over the rough edges of the wood. The sand on the paper wears away all the splinters and uneven spots and leaves the wood smooth and clean.

"That's what a good friend is like. They help you rub away all the rough edges and help you get past things you do that could hurt other people by lovingly showing you how to be a better friend!" Proverbs 27:17 says, *"As iron sharpens iron, so a friend sharpens a friend."*

So, your relationships help you grow, your relationships help rub off the rough edges of your life, and lastly:

 ## 3. YOUR RELATIONSHIPS HELP YOU THROUGH HARD STUFF.

Kendal was going through a tough time with his family. His parents were fighting a lot and his brother and sister were really busy with all of their friends and activities. Kendall felt lonely and sad, and he wasn't sure what to do.

One day his friend Carter noticed that something was wrong. He asked Kendall if he was okay, and suddenly everything that had been bothering him came rushing out. He told Carter all the things he was feeling and how worried he was about everything. As he shared what was going on in his life, suddenly the weight that had been on him didn't seem quite so heavy anymore.

The people in your life can help get you through the hard things that we all face. Your parents can help you work through a tough season with your friends. Your teachers can help you overcome some fears you might have at school. Your friends can stand beside you when you're facing all kinds of things and remind you you're not alone. Proverbs 17:17 says, *"A friend is always loyal, and a brother is born to help in time of need."*

God doesn't want us to go through life alone. He gave us other people to walk through our lives with us. That's one of His best gifts, and we want to make sure we take really, really good care of those relationships.

Closing Prayer: *Dear God, Thank You for the amazing gift of relationships. Thank You for blessing me with friends and family who will walk through my life with me. Help me treat people the way I want to be treated and take good care of all the relationships in my life. I love You. Amen.*

DOODLE PAGE

God has given us a "Super-Secret Weapon" when it comes to knowing how to handle the relationships in our lives. On the rocket below, write out the names of your friends, family, and other people in your life. See **HOW MANY** names you can fit in the space! Then remember to treat them the way **YOU** want to be treated!

TREAT PEOPLE IN THE SAME WAY THAT YOU WANT THEM TO TREAT YOU.

—Luke 6:31 (CEB)

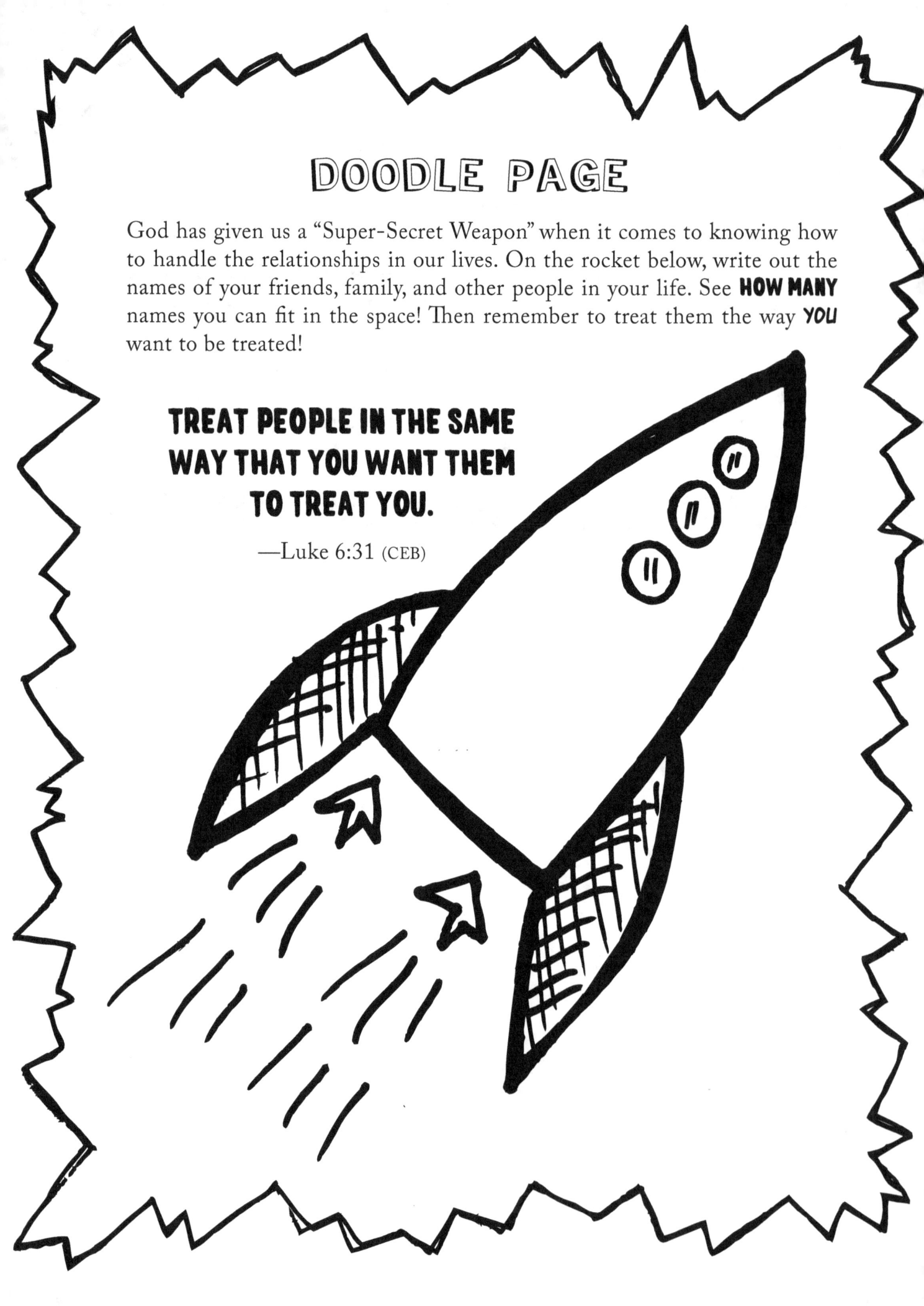

ACTIVITY SHEET

WEEK 1

God created us to share our lives with other people. In the frames, draw and color the following pictures:

You and your parents

You and your favorite teacher

You and your best friend

The first two companions, Adam and Eve

Fill in the missing letters to reveal the verse.

Tre ___t

peo___le

___n

t___e

sam___

___ay

t___at

___ou

wa___t

th___m

___o

tre___t

y___u.

—Luke 6:31 (CEB)

Bazooka Boys ★ Relationships

Find the highlighted words in each verse in the puzzle below (all Scripture NIV).

Do to **others** as you **would** have them do to you (Luke 6:31).

The **LORD** God formed the man from the **dust** of the **ground** and **breathed** into his **nostrils** the breath of **life**, and the man became a **living** being (Genesis 2:7).

The LORD **God** said, "It is not **good** for the man to be **alone**. I will make a **helper** suitable for him (Genesis 2:18).

Wounds from a **friend** can be **trusted**, but an enemy multiplies **kisses** (Proverbs 27:6).

As **iron** sharpens iron, so one man **sharpens** another (Proverbs 27:17).

```
D D L M T B D G Y T G O L U A
R K E C K N K R W E O G N T S
O E H T E Z S O T R D S I N A
L T Y I S G U U L Z A X E L S
K I R J M U A N K A C P V C B
Y F R S X U R D S E R E H V R
B Q L O M E K T X A W F I L E
X J X O N M N I H R A I B E A
Q R N O U M S S S N E L M R T
V T L W J F O W E S S P Y N H
E A U W Q V R F O R E N L V E
S L I R T S O N E U P S U E D
L I V I N G E H D H L U S H H
C L G O O D T A Q Z O D P B U
I F Y P N O G D U S T X V D Y
```

Step 1: Read each verse below and find the missing word (all Scripture NIV).

Do to (1) _____ as you would have them do to you (Luke 6:31).

The LORD God formed the man from the dust of the ground and breathed into his nostrils the (2) _____ of life, and the man became a living being (Genesis 2:7).

The LORD God said, "It is not good for the man to be (3) _____. I will make a helper suitable for him (Genesis 2:18).

Wounds from a friend can be (4) _____, but an enemy multiplies kisses (Proverbs 27:6).

As iron (5) _____ iron, so one man sharpens another (Proverbs 27:17).

Step 2: Fill in the missing word from each verse above with the corresponding number.

1. ____   2. ____   5. ____
   ____   ____   ____
   ____   ____   ____
   ____   ____   ____
   ____   ____   4. ____   ____
   ____   ____   3. ____   ____   ____
                       ____   ____   ____
                       ____   ____   ____
                       ____   ____   ____
                       ____
                       ____

Step 3: Discover what God wants us to do with our lives.

God created us to ____ ____ ____ ____ ____ our lives with other people.

Bazooka Boys ★ Relationships

BAZOOKA BREAKDOWN

WEEK 1

God brings all kinds of special people into our lives. Write about someone who is very special to you. Why is that person important to you? Glue a picture of them here or draw a picture of them instead!

God gives us relationships to help us grow. Is there someone in your life who has taught you something or helped you realize something you are good at? Write about it here.

Our relationships can also help "rub off the rough edges" in our lives. That means they help us see things in our lives that need to change. On the piece of wood below, write out some things that friends or family have helped you change for the better!

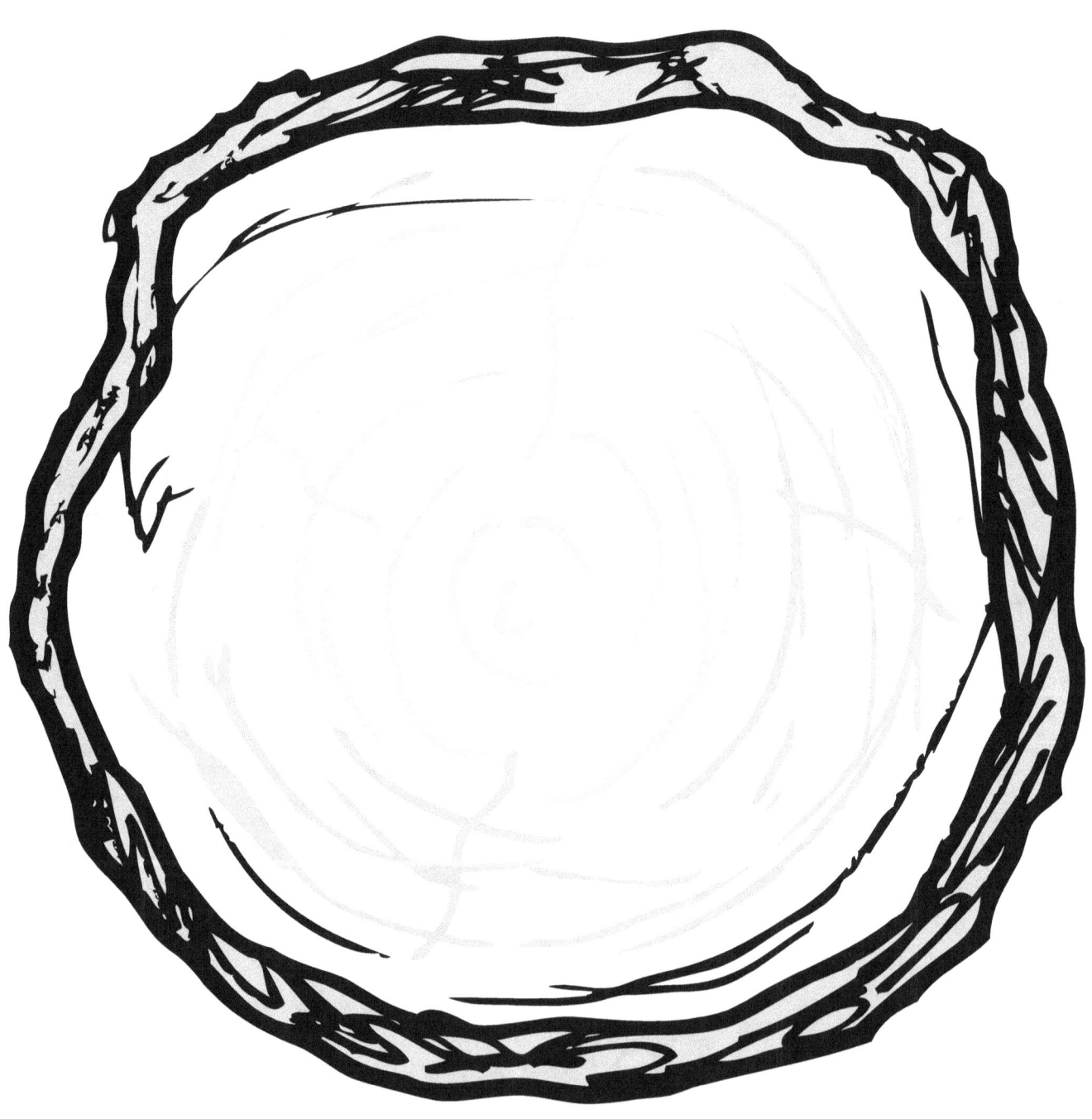

Bazooka Boys ★ Relationships

Write out this verse three times and see if you can memorize it!

"Treat people in the same way that you want them to treat you."
—Luke 6:31 (CEB)

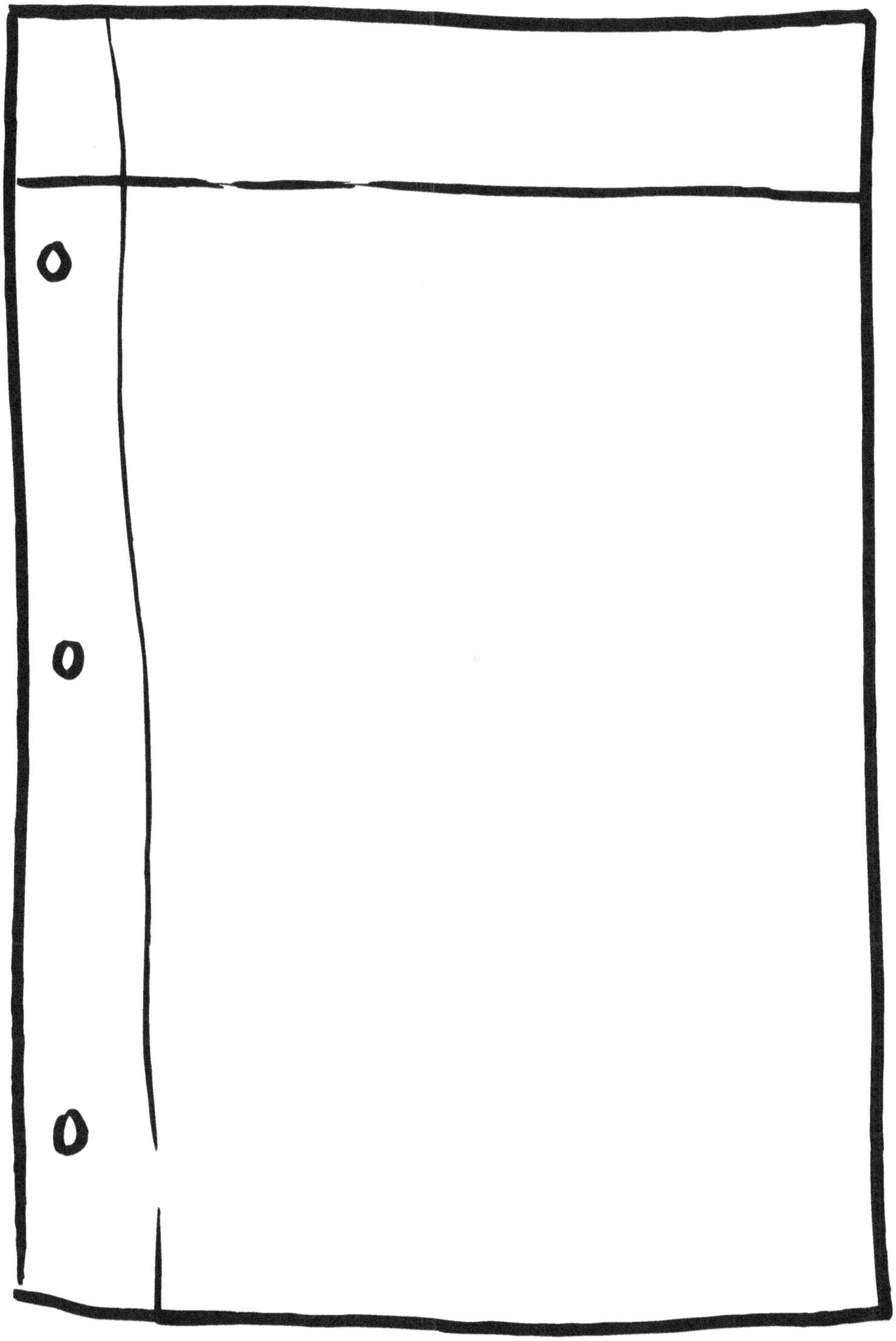

Bazooka Boys ★ Relationships

OPTION 1: EXPERIMENT - BALLOON ROCKETS

(20 minutes)

<u>Supplies</u>

- Balloon(s)
- Long piece of string (approximately 10 feet)
- Drinking straw(s)
- Masking Tape

<u>What Should We Do Next?</u>

1. Thread the string through the straw

2. Hook your piece of string between two chairs or objects with one end of the string higher than the other end.

3. Blow up the balloon but do NOT tie it off, just keep it pinched shut.

4. Without letting the balloon deflate, tape the straw to the top of the balloon with masking tape. Have a friend help you to ensure the rocket does not deflate before launch.

5. Slide the straw and balloon up to the high end of the string.

6. Let go! Watch your balloon rocket shoot to the end of the string.

Energy is released when the air rushes out of the balloon. This energy then creates something called thrust that propels the balloon forward. Just like the balloon, we need people in our lives that will push us forward rather than deflate our spirits.

OPTION 2: SANDPAPER ART

(20 minutes)

Supplies

- Sandpaper (60 grit or 100 grit)
- Crayons

Prep

- Cut sandpaper into 5" x 7" or 8" x 11" sizes, depending on the age and skill level of the boys.
- Put the sandpaper picture face up on a towel.
- Place a piece of white cardstock (or white T-shirt) on top of the picture and a paper towel or thin cloth on top of that.
- Using a warm iron, iron over the picture for about 15 seconds.
- Carefully lift up the cardstock (or T-shirt) to reveal your picture. The picture will reveal a cool dot effect.
- Look at the sandpaper art. You'll notice the crayon wax melted onto the grains of sand in the sandpaper, creating a smooth, finished effect.

What Should We Do Next?

1. Using crayons, color a cool picture on the sandpaper. Tip: Remember to write any word or words backwards so they'll transfer correctly onto white cardstock or T-shirt.

2. Press hard with the crayons to get a nice layer of color.

3. Each picture should cover the entire piece of sandpaper, so make sure you color the background, too.

FRIENDSHIP

WHAT'S THE POINT?
IF WE WANT TO HAVE GOOD FRIENDS, WE MUST BE A GOOD FRIEND.

THEME VERSE:
A man that hath friends must show himself friendly.
Proverbs 18:34 (KJ21)

RELATED BIBLE PASSAGE:
Ruth and Naomi
Ruth 1

There's **NOTHING** like a really good friend. You know, the kind of friend you can laugh with until your face hurts and your stomach aches. The kind you can go on the craziest, most awesome adventures with and you know they're always up for anything. The kind that just **KNOW** when you're having a bad day and give you their extra Oreos at lunch just to make you feel better.

Good friends are gifts from God. He loves to bless us with people who make our lives better. God gives us friends so we have can have fun together! He gives us friends to support and encourage us when we're going through hard times. He gives us friends to challenge us and inspire us to grow. And God gives us friends so we know we're not alone in this life.

Our friendships are something we should take really good care of. The Bible tells that if we want to **HAVE** good friends, we must **BE** a good friend. Proverbs 18:24 says, *"A man that hath friends must show himself friendly..."* (KJ21). This means we need to take the time and effort to make sure that we're being a good friend.

Remember God's super-secret weapon for relationships? Treat other people the way you want to be treated. You should BE the kind of friend that you would want to have.

What are some ways you can be a good friend?

 ## 1. BE A LOYAL FRIEND.

What does it mean to be loyal? A loyal friend is someone you can count on. Someone you KNOW will be there for you no matter what. Someone who has your back no matter what you may face.

Being loyal means that your friends know they can count on you. If something is going on in their lives, they know you will be there for them. If other people are saying bad things about you, a loyal friend will stick up for you. No matter what, you're confident they have your back.

Bazooka Boys ★ Relationships

Have you ever had a really loyal friend? Someone who was always there for you no matter what? There's nothing quite as comforting as knowing there's someone sticking up for you. It's such a good feeling to know there are people who will always be there for you and stand up for you.

Have you ever had a friend who wasn't loyal? The kind of friend who will be your friend one day and then the next day they're a jerk to you? Or maybe you've had a friend who says, "I'm not going to be your friend anymore," if you don't do what they want you to do? Loyal friends don't say, "I'm not going to be your friend anymore." Loyal friends may have disagreements, but they never threaten to take away their friendship.

I remember a friend I had when I was younger who was NOT a very loyal friend. It seemed like he was always ticked off at me for one reason or another. It took me a long time to realize it, but he wasn't a very good friend. After a lot of frustration, I finally decided to spend my time on the friends who were loyal to me. I was still nice to him, but I learned that he just couldn't be a really close friend because I couldn't trust him.

Maybe you haven't been a very loyal friend. Maybe you haven't been consistent with the friends in your life. Today is the day you can start being a loyal friend. Decide you're going to be there for your friends no matter what. When you get

frustrated with them, talk it through, but never threaten to take your friendship away. Fill your friends with the confidence that comes from knowing that you'll be there for them.

God wants you to be a **LOYAL** friend. Proverbs 17:7 says, "*A friend is always loyal.*" If you want to be a good friend, be a loyal friend.

The second way you can be a good friend is to

 ## 2. BE AN ENCOURAGER

Have you ever had a friend in your life who made you feel like you could do anything? You know, the kind of friend who tells you to **GO FOR IT** and cheers you on along the way? An encouraging friend is someone who helps you believe in yourself. They're the friends who tell you all the things you're good at. They pat you on the back and are proud of you when you do well.

Sam had the most encouraging friend **EVER**. His name was Abel. No matter what he was doing, Abel was always there for him. When he decided to audition for the jazz band at school, he was SO nervous he thought he was going to puke! But Sam called him and **TOTALLY** encouraged him. He said, "Sam, you are **SO** good—you're going to do **AWESOME** at your audition. I know you're going to be amazing!" Sam couldn't believe how much stronger he felt after his friend spoke encouraging words to him.

1 Thessalonians 5:11 says, "*So encourage each other and build each other up.*" God wants us to help each other feel better about ourselves. We should be pointing out all the **GOOD** things about our friends and encouraging them!

Bazooka Boys ★ Relationships

But sometimes it can be hard to be encouraging. Why is that? Sometimes, when our friends do really well at something, we can feel jealous. Or when our friends do something really amazing, it makes us feel bad about ourselves because **WE** didn't do something as amazing as them. But those are all silly reasons not to encourage our friends, right?

The truth is, just because someone else is successful, doesn't mean WE won't be successful too! Seeing our friends do well should be something that fills us with joy, not jealousy. Helping our friends feel better about themselves is an awesome thing to do.

Have you ever helped light the candles on a birthday cake? Sometimes people use one candle that is lit to light the other candles that aren't lit. Let me ask you a question. When you use one candle to light another, does anything bad happen to the first candle? Does is make the flame any smaller? Does the fire go out when it helps spread the light? **NO!**

When we encourage our friends, when we hope for the best for them, when we tell them how amazing and awesome they are, it doesn't take anything away from us. When your friends succeed, it doesn't mean **YOU** won't be successful. When you light someone else's candle with your kind and encouraging words, your light stays just as bright. And now there are two of you lighting the world instead of just one!

Be an encourager. When you notice a friend doing something well, tell them! When someone is nervous about trying something new, let them know you believe in them and they can do it! Be your friend's biggest supporter.

2 Corinthians 13:11 says, "*Encourage each other. Live in harmony and peace. Then the God of love and peace will be with you.*"

So, be a good friend by being loyal, encouraging, and lastly,

 ## 3. DON't BE A SELFISH FRIEND.

Oh my, it can be SO easy to think about the things **WE** want! The things **WE** want to play. The things **WE** want to do. The things **WE** want our friends to do. The things **WE DON'T** want our friends to do.

But a good friend doesn't just think about the things they want, they think about their friends! Philippians 2:3 says, *"Don't be selfish; don't try to impress others. Be humble, thinking of others as better than yourselves."* This means we aren't supposed to only think about the things WE want, but we should think about our friends, too!

There's a story in the Bible about a person who did something **AMAZINGLY** unselfish for her friend. Her name was Ruth, and she was a very good friend to her mother-in-law, Naomi. All of Naomi's family had died, so she decided to move away from where she was living, back to the home of her ancestors. Her daughter-in-law, Ruth, decided to go with her so she wouldn't be alone.

This was a **HUGE** deal. Ruth would have to leave all her family and friends and move to a new country where she didn't know anyone! But she knew her mother-in-law would really need her, so she was willing to go. She thought about Naomi's feelings and needs far above her own. In Ruth 1:16 she says, *"Wherever you go, I will go; wherever you live, I will live. Your people will be my people and your God will be my God."*

I can imagine that it would have been a difficult decision for Ruth. But she thought about what was best for Naomi, and how she could help and support her instead of what might be easiest for her. Ruth was a very unselfish friend.

God wants you to think about other people's feelings, not just your own. He wants you to consider ways you can encourage and bless the people in your life, not just think about what YOU want all the time.

Don't you think it would be SO cool if we all could simply be the kind of friend that we want to have? A friend who is loyal no matter what? A friend who encourages us and cheers us on? A friend who isn't selfish but thinks of what's best for the other people in their life?

I want those kind of friends. And I want to be that kind of friend.

Closing Prayer: *Dear God, thank You for the gift of friendship. I pray that You will help me be the best friend possible. Help me be loyal, encouraging, and unselfish toward the friends in my life. I love You. Amen.*

ACTIVITY SHEET

WEEK 2

Draw a picture of you and your best friend!

Don't be afraid to root for your friends! You should be their biggest supporters and greatest encouragers.

In the text bubbles below, write the name of each your friends and one thing you think is really cool about them. Encourage them this week by sharing what you wrote.

Bazooka Boys ★ Relationships

WEEK 2

Read the following verses about friendship in your Bible and find the missing word (all Scripture NIV).

A friend _____ at all times... (Proverbs 17:17).

Perfume and incense bring _____ to the heart, and the pleasantness of one's friend springs from his earnest counsel (Proverbs 27:9).

Live in harmony with one another. Do not be _____, but be willing to associate with people of low position. Do not be _____ (Romans 12:16).

Therefore _____ one another and build each other up, just as in fact you are doing (1 Thessalonians 5:11).

Do nothing out of _____ ambition or vain conceit, but in humility consider others better than yourselves (Philippians 2:3).

Word List

encourage	*joy*	*selfish*
conceited	*loves*	*proud*

Things about us! Fill out this survey with a friend.

	You	Me
1. Favorite food		
2. Favorite movie		
3. Favorite book		
4. If you could be an animal, what would it be?		
5. What word best describes you?		
6. If you could go anywhere in the world, where would you go?		

                                                                You   Me

7. Name one great thing about your family.

8. Favorite season

9. Favorite singer

10. What are you afraid of?

11. If you won a million dollars, what would you do with it?

12. Favorite animal

13. If you could change your name, what would it be?

14. What do you like better?

    a. Candy or chips

    b. Dogs or cats

    c. Sports or Music

    d. Reading or Drawing

    e. Board games or computer games

    f. Camping or hotels

    g. Sweat pants or jeans

    k. On stage or behind the scenes

    l. Winter or summer

    m. Hunting or fishing

    n. Biking or skateboarding

    o. Football or Baseball

    p. Soccer or hockey

15. What will I be doing in 10 years?

16. Will we be friends forever?

Bazooka Boys ★ Relationships

Ruth & Naomi: Friends Forever!

Read Ruth 1:16–18 (NIV) in the Bible and find the missing word. Find those same words in the word search puzzle.

¹⁶But _____ replied, "Don't urge me to _____ you or to turn back from you. Where you _____ I will go, and where you _____ I will stay. Your _____ will be my people and your _____ my God. ¹⁷Where you _____ I will die, and there I will be _____. May the _____ deal with me, be it ever so severely, if anything but death _____ you and me." 18 When _____ realized that Ruth was _____ to go with her, she stopped urging her.

```
s e p a r a t e s e o b
o l n g b n i o v l l u
g p o s t a y h d i e r
n o d r e o l t o e a i
t e d p d m i u m e v e
l p d e n i m r e t e d
```

Word List

Ruth	stay	buried	Naomi
leave	people	Lord	determined
go	God	separates	die

BAZOOKA BREAKDOWN

Look up the word **LOYAL** in the dictionary and write the definition here. How can you be a **LOYAL** friend?

LOYAL:

Bazooka Boys ★ Relationships

It feels pretty nice when someone encourages you! It makes you feel strong and confident. On the superhero's arms, write out some things that people have said about you that have encouraged you!

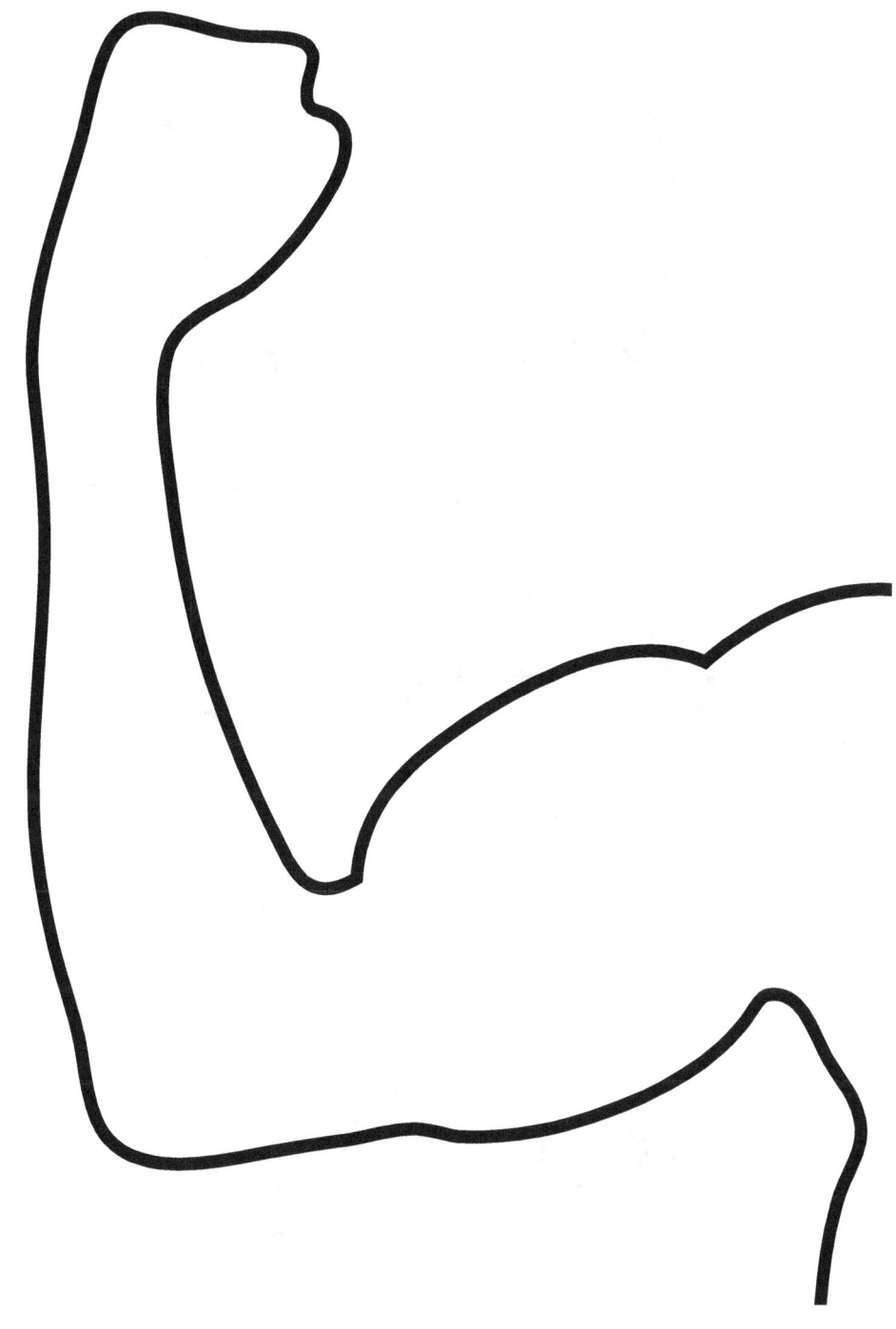

God doesn't want us to be a selfish friend. What are some ways that you can think of others instead of yourself? Make a list of five things you can do to think of others before yourself.

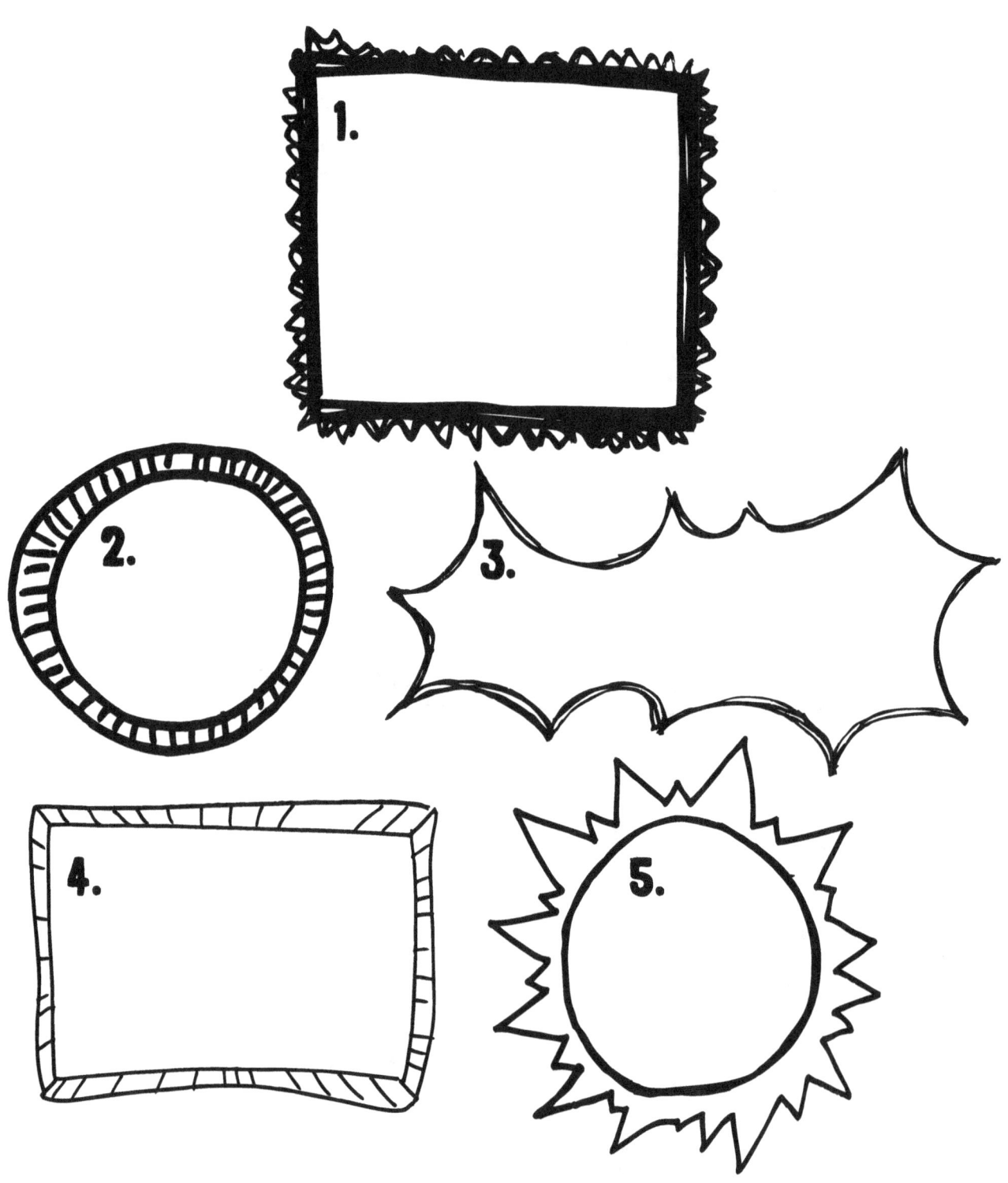

Bazooka Boys ★ Relationships

Write out this verse three times and see if you can memorize it!

"A man that hath friends must show himself friendly..."
—Proverbs 18:24 (KJ21)

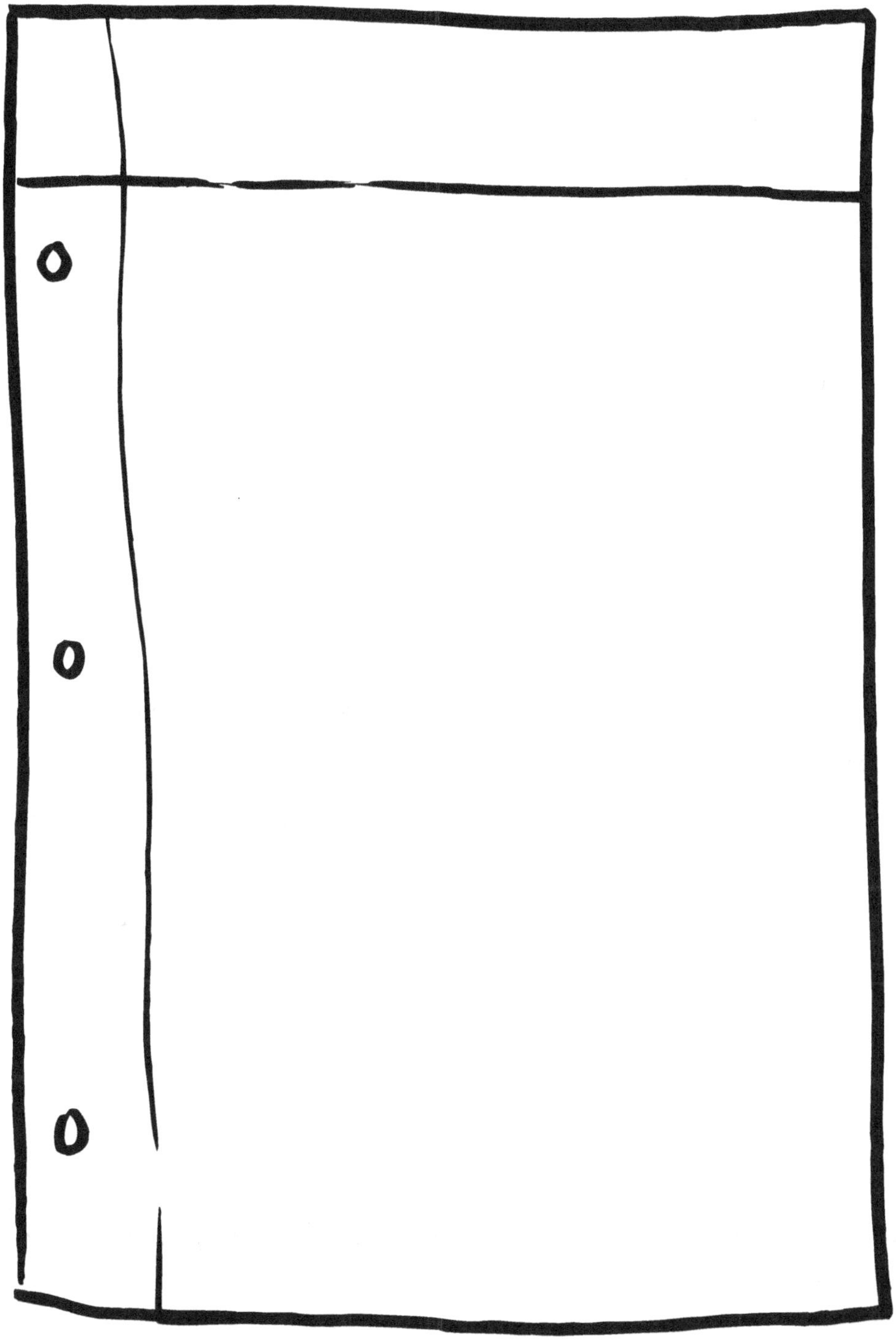

OPTION 1: MARSHMALLOW CATAPULT

(20 minutes)

Supplies

- 4 large marshmallows
- 7 bamboo skewers
- 1 thin rubber band
- 1 spoon
- Masking tape
- Scissors

Parent Prep

- Have your parents trim the points off of each skewer for safety.

What should we do next?

1. Using three marshmallows and three skewers, form a triangle on a flat surface.
2. Use three more skewers and one more marshmallow to form another pyramid on top of the triangle
3. Tape the plastic spoon securely to the last skewer with masking tape.
4. Loop the rubber band around the topmost marshmallow
5. Insert the spoon skewer through the rubber band into one of the base marshmallows.
6. Make a target.
7. Place a small object in the spoon, pull back the spoon against the rubber band, and release!

Bazooka Boys ★ Relationships

OPTION 2: MINI BOW AND ARROW

(20 minutes)

Supplies

- Popsicle Sticks
- Bowl of water
- Fishing line or dental floss
- Scissors
- Craft knife (adults only)
- Hot glue (optional, adults only)
- Q-Tips (3 per boy)

Prep

- Soak Popsicle sticks in water for at least two hours. The soaking makes the sticks soft and bendable.
- Using your craft knife, have your parent cut four small notches in each Popsicle stick—two notches on each end.
- After the sticks are done soaking, gently bend them into a bow shape. Start in the middle and work your way to each end. If the stick breaks, then continue soaking the rest until they're more pliable.
- When the stick is bent, tie the line to one end using the notches to keep it on the stick.
- Using a craft knife, have your parent make a notch at the end of each Q-tip. The notch will be help you line up the arrow (Q-tip)

What Should We Do Next?

1. Attach the line to the Popsicle stick.
   - Wrap the line around the first end a couple times.
   - Bring the line down to the other end.
   - Wrap it around that end a couple times.
   - Bring the line back around the other side and tie it off.
2. Place a dab of hot glue on each end to secure the line (optional).
3. Shoot your arrows!

Bazooka Boys ★ Relationships

MY FAMILY

WHAT'S THE POINT?
HONOR YOUR PARENTS, BE KIND TO YOUR FAMILY, AND STICK TOGETHER.

THEME VERSE:
I pray that the Lord will let your family and your descendants always grow strong.
Psalm 115:14 (CEV)

RELATED BIBLE PASSAGE:
Joab and Abishai
1 Chronicles 19

They see your best and they know your worst. They're the people who mean the most to you, and the people who can drive you nutty the fastest. The people you would stick up for to anyone, anywhere, over anything—but also the people you spend the most time fighting, arguing with, and getting crazy mad at. They're the ones who can make you feel the best about yourself, but sometimes they're the people who can say things that make you feel bad, too. Who are these loony people?

YOUR FAMILY.

Earlier we talked about the fact that God gives us people to walk through life with—and there's NO one closer to us on our journey than our families. They're the ones we live with and spend the most time around.

God gives us families to help us in countless ways. Do you remember being a baby? Really? I don't either. But your parents were the ones who cared for you when you were a baby. They changed your diapers (yuck!) and mushed up your food (gross!) and made sure you were well taken care of. As you grew older, they showed you how to do things, taught you all the stuff you needed to learn, and made sure that you were always safe.

Now, your mom and dad do their best to teach you all the things you need to learn in order to become the best person you can possibly be. They're not perfect and will make lots of mistakes, but they love you and want the best for you… even if sometimes they don't do everything perfectly.

We also have other people in our families—brothers and sisters and cousins and grandparents and lots of other people who are all part of our families. Some people have really big families and some people have really small families. Some family members live really close to each other and spend a lot of time together, and some family members don't really spend much time together at all. No matter what your family may look like, God has some instructions for you for dealing with the people in your family.

First of all, God gives us some very important instructions when it comes to how we treat our parents:

 ## 1. WE NEED TO HONOR OUR PARENTS.

There are quite a few places in the Bible where we find this very specific direction. Ephesians 6:1–3 says, *"Children, obey your parents because you belong to the Lord, for this is the right thing to do. Honor your father and mother. This is the first commandment with a promise: If you honor your father and mother, things will go well for you, and you will have a long life on the earth."*

What does it mean to **HONOR** our parents? Honoring someone means respecting them. It means obeying them and doing what they ask of you. It means speaking to them in a way that isn't disrespectful or rude. When you honor someone, you're thanking them for the special role they play in your life.

You see, God has given you to your parents as their responsibility. When you honor them by doing what they ask, speaking respectfully, and having an attitude of appreciation toward them, you're honoring the role God has given them in your life. When you honor your parents, you're really honoring God!

Sometimes it can be hard to honor your parents. There are moments when they frustrate you. There are times you simply don't want to do what they say. And sometimes, you don't understand why they want you to do the things they want you to do. But no matter what, you need to **HONOR** them.

Not only does it please God when we act that way, there's a reward for us when we follow this very important rule! Actually, this is the first commandment in the Bible that comes with a promise. God makes a deal with us. He says, "If you will honor your parents and treat them with respect, then I am going to help things to go well for you." I think that's a pretty good deal!

You need to work really hard to honor your parents. When you feel like ignoring what they tell you to do, remember God wants you to honor them by obeying. When you start to say something rude, stop yourself and remember God wants you to speak respectfully to your parents. When you're tempted to treat your parents poorly or have a bad attitude, ask God to help you honor them even when it's difficult.

Sometimes you might think, "Well, I'm frustrated with my Mom and Dad, so I don't have to honor them." You know what? God doesn't tell us that we only need to honor our parents if we like the things they're telling us to do. He doesn't tell us that we only have to honor our parents when we feel like it. The Bible tells us that it's our responsibility to keep our attitudes respectful and honoring. It doesn't depend on their behavior toward us, or whether we feel like they've earned it. God wants you to honor your parents no matter what.

Just So You Know: There are a lot of situations that make it really difficult to honor your parents. Sometimes your parents can go through a hard time and may treat you in a way they shouldn't. If you're ever scared by something your mom or dad is doing, it's really important that you talk to someone about it. Share your concerns with a teacher, another family member, a friend, or even your pastor. When you seek help for your mom or dad when they need it, you're honoring them in a really special way. You're respecting them enough to get help, and God will be really, really proud of you.

So, God wants you to HONOR your parents.

Another thing God wants you to do is:

 ## 2. BE KIND tO YOUR FAMILY.

Kindness, hmm. Seems easy enough, right? Of course we all know we should be kind to each other, but sometimes it can be really hard to be kind to the people closest to us.

Bazooka Boys ★ Relationships

Joe has a sister named Heather. Joe loves her, but he's not so sure how much he likes her. She can really, really get on his nerves. Sometimes, she does things just to bother him and no matter what he says, she just won't stop. After a while, Joe finds himself **EXPLODING** at his sister. He screams and yells and sometimes he even wants to hit her!

What's so crazy is that Joe would **NEVER** think of screaming or yelling or wanting to hit one of his friends. Even if they made him super mad, he wouldn't think of treating a friend that way.

Sometimes we treat our families differently than we would ever treat our friends. We're a lot less cautious about the things we say and do with the people closest to us. It's easy to forget our brothers and sisters and other family members have feelings just like our friends.

God wants you to be kind to your family. Even if they're driving you crazy. Even if you're so frustrated you just want to scream. Even if they're not kind to you. 2 Timothy 2:24 says, "*A servant of the Lord must not quarrel but must be kind to everyone, be able to teach, and be patient with difficult people.*" (Yes, your little sister will fall into the category of "difficult people" sometimes!)

You must be kind to your family. Don't say mean things to your brother or sister. Don't tease them. Don't make fun of them. Don't react when they're trying to get you angry. When you feel like you're going to lose it and say something **UNKIND**, stop yourself and remember God wants us to be kind to one another. Maybe you'll need to walk away and take a few minutes to calm yourself down. Maybe you'll need to go talk to your mom or dad about the situation. Or maybe you just need to smile at them and tell them you love them!

You'll never regret the moments when you're kind to other people. Even if they don't deserve it, you'll know you made the right choice in choosing kindness.

And the last way God wants you to treat your family, is to

 **3. STICK TOGETHER.**

Remember when we talked about loyalty? Being loyal means you stand by someone no matter what. There's no place loyalty is more important than in your family.

God didn't make a mistake when He put you in the family you're in. He did it for a reason. He gave you your family so you would have someone to walk through life with you—to help you, support you, and have your back.

There's a story in the Bible about two brothers who had each other's backs. Joab was the leader of the army for King David. He had to fight all kinds of bad guys who were trying to destroy the nation of Israel. Joab was facing a tough situation. There were people ahead of him wanting to fight him, and there were people behind him who wanted to fight him. He was surrounded! So you know what he did? He called on his brother to help him. 1 Chronicles 19:10–13 says, *"When Joab saw that he had two fronts to fight, before and behind, he took his pick of the best of Israel and deployed them to confront the Arameans. The rest of the army he put under the command of Abishai, his brother, and deployed them to deal with the Ammonites. Then he said, 'If the Arameans are too much for me, you help me; and if the Ammonites prove too much for you, I'll come and help you. Courage!'"*

Did you read that? These brothers had each other's backs! If one of them needed help, he knew his brother would be there for them. If he was in trouble, his family would fight for him. Joab could confidently go into battle knowing that his brother was right by his side.

We know in our hearts that we should be there for our families, but sometimes we get so busy with all the things we're doing—hanging out with friends, going to activities, playing with cool new toys—that we can forget that part of our job is to be there for the people in our families.

Maybe your brother or sister is having a hard time and they don't have anyone to talk to. Would they feel comfortable coming to you with their problems? Would they feel like you would listen to them or help them?

Bazooka Boys ★ Relationships

Or would they feel like you would tell them to leave you alone so you could do other things?

If your mom was having a really busy week and she was totally overwhelmed, could she count on you to help her with the chores around the house and to help clean up? Or would you react with a million excuses about why it's not fair that you have to help?

Families stick together. They help each other out. They work together as a team to help each person succeed.

Your family is a team. When you only think about yourself and what you want and what you're doing, you're never going to get anywhere. But when you decide to work together and think of ways you can help each other out, your family will grow stronger and you'll be stronger individuals, too!

Families are a gift from God. He blessed you with people who love you, care about you, and want to help you do the very best you can. Don't take your family for granted…but do your best to treat them with all the love and respect you can. Yes, even your annoying little sister.

Closing Prayer: *Dear God, thank You for my family. I know they're a special treasure from You, and I am so grateful for them. Show me how I can honor my mom and dad. Help me show kindness to my family members, even when it's hard. And teach me ways that I can support my family and help us work together as a team. I love You, Jesus. Amen.*

DOODLE PAGE

LESSON 3

In the space provided, draw a picture of each of your family members. Then think of something cool or unique about each person and give them a superhero name that goes with that trait. Write their name above their picture!

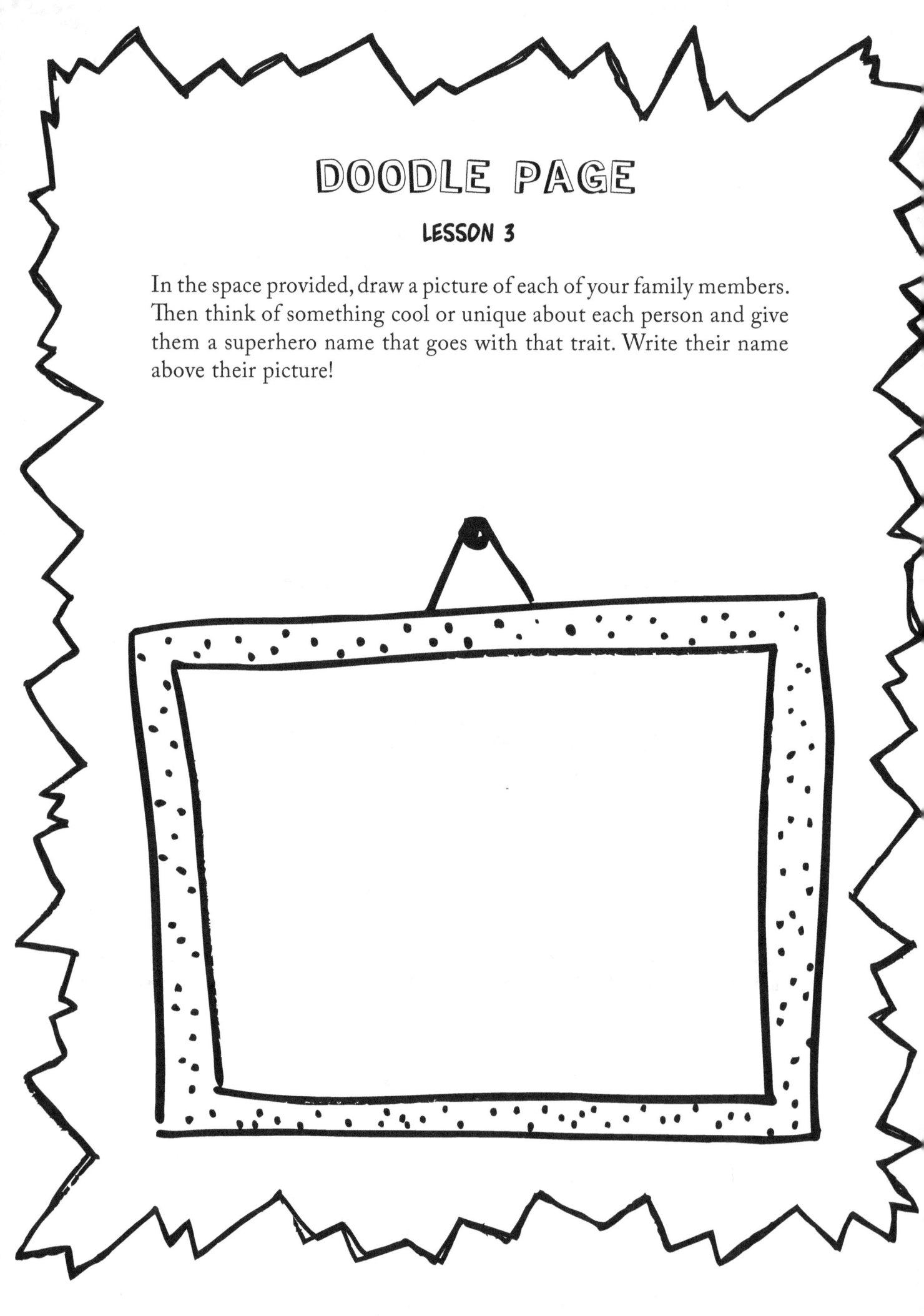

ACTIVITY SHEET

WEEK 3

2 Timothy 2:24 says *"A servant of the Lord must not quarrel but must **BE** kind to everyone, **BE** able to teach, and **BE** patient with difficult people."*

Fill in the blanks with the word **KIND**. Look up each verse in your Bible (all Scripture NIV).

Love is patient, love is _____. It does not envy, it does not boast, it is not proud (1 Corinthians 13:4).

But the fruit of the Spirit is love, joy, peace, patience, _____ ness, goodness, faithfulness… (Galatians 5:22).

Be _____ and compassionate to one another, forgiving each other, just as in Christ God forgave you (Ephesians 4:32).

Make sure that nobody pays back wrong for wrong, but always try to be _____ to each other and to everyone else (1 Thessalonians 5:15).

49

God gives us people in our world to walk through our lives together. And there is **NO** one closer to us on our journey than our families. Find the words from the list in the Word Search Puzzle.

Word Search Puzzle

```
I P A R A S Y R T H A T T H G
E R P T S S E N D N I K P O P
T O P L O S O L R D W A D A I
Y N R R P G L K C I T S R J L
L O E E A L E E T I Y E O O U
I H C M R Y F T E A N A M I L
M T I O D Y A N H T B O N D Y
A Y A B O N C U S E R D R T E
F S T E C E A E N D R A L H N
T S E Y A L W M A Y S A G R C
A B I S H A I O M W Y S T R O
N G L I E J B C K O D O D S M
E P S K S M X R L O C E I G Q
```

Word List

abishai
joab
appreciate
chronicles
commandment
family

God
honor
kindness
loyalty
obey
parents

patience
pray
respect
stick
together

Bazooka Boys ★ Relationships

No matter what your family looks like, God has some instructions for you for dealing with the people in your family.

Unscramble the words to reveal God's instructions.

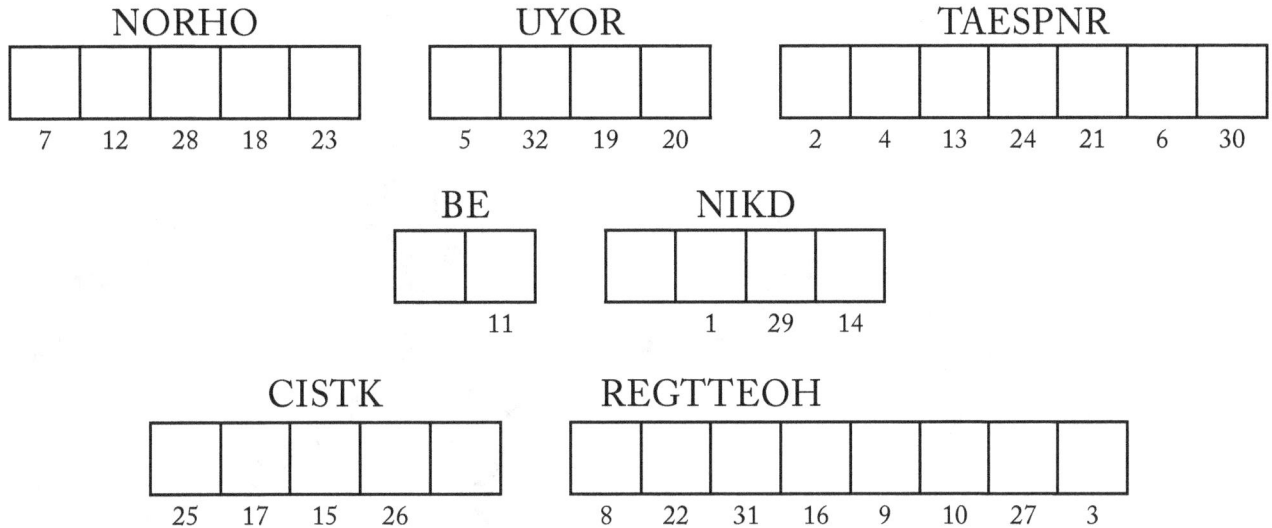

Copy the letters in the numbered cells to other cells with the same number to reveal God's Word.

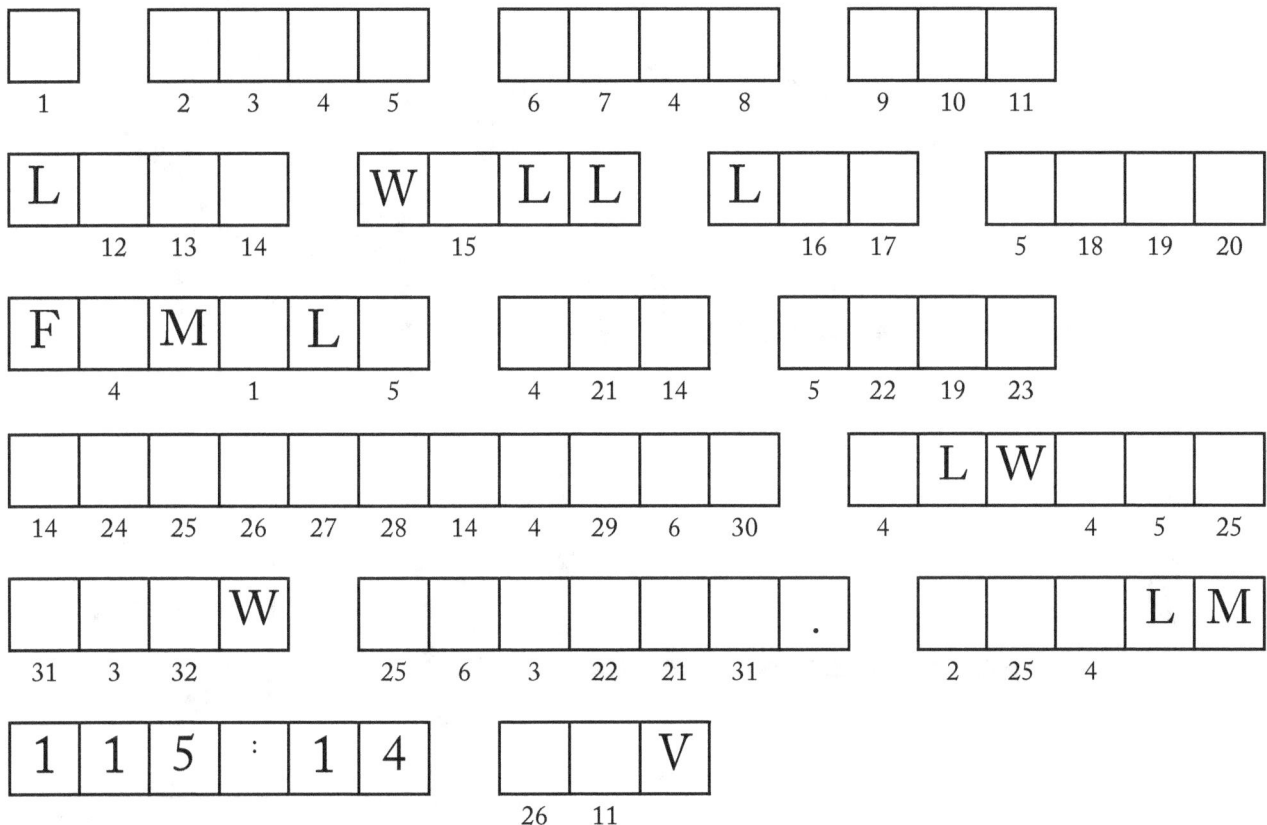

BAZOOKA BREAKDOWN

God wants us to treat our families with kindness. Why do you think it's so hard to be kind to our families sometimes? Write out your thoughts in the space provided

Bazooka Boys ★ Relationships

WEEK 3

What are some specific ways you can be kind to your family? Think of one thing you can do for each person in your family and write it in the space provided.

Name _____

-

-

-

Name _____

-

-

-

Name _____

-

-

-

Name _____

-

-

-

Name _____

-

-

-

I'VE GOT YOUR BACK!

Families stick together. What does it mean to "have someone's back?" Read the pledge below, write your name in the space provided and sign it to pledge to always watch out for your family. Then have the members of your family sign the pledge as well!

I, _____,

promise to always have your back.

I promise to watch out for you, take care of you,
and help you when you need help.

Signed _____

Date _____

I, _____,

promise to always have your back.

I promise to watch out for you, take care of you,
and help you when you need help.

Signed _____

Date _____

I, _____,

promise to always have your back.

I promise to watch out for you, take care of you,
and help you when you need help.

Signed _____

Date _____

I, _____,

promise to always have your back.

I promise to watch out for you, take care of you,
and help you when you need help.

Signed _____

Date _____

I, _____,

promise to always have your back.

I promise to watch out for you, take care of you,
and help you when you need help.

Signed _____

Date _____

I, _____,

promise to always have your back.

I promise to watch out for you, take care of you, and help you when you need help.

Signed _____

Date _____

I, _____,

promise to always have your back.

I promise to watch out for you, take care of you, and help you when you need help.

Signed _____

Date _____

Write out the following verse three times and see if you can memorize it!

"I pray that the Lord will let your family and your descendants always grow strong."
—Psalm 115:14 (CEV)

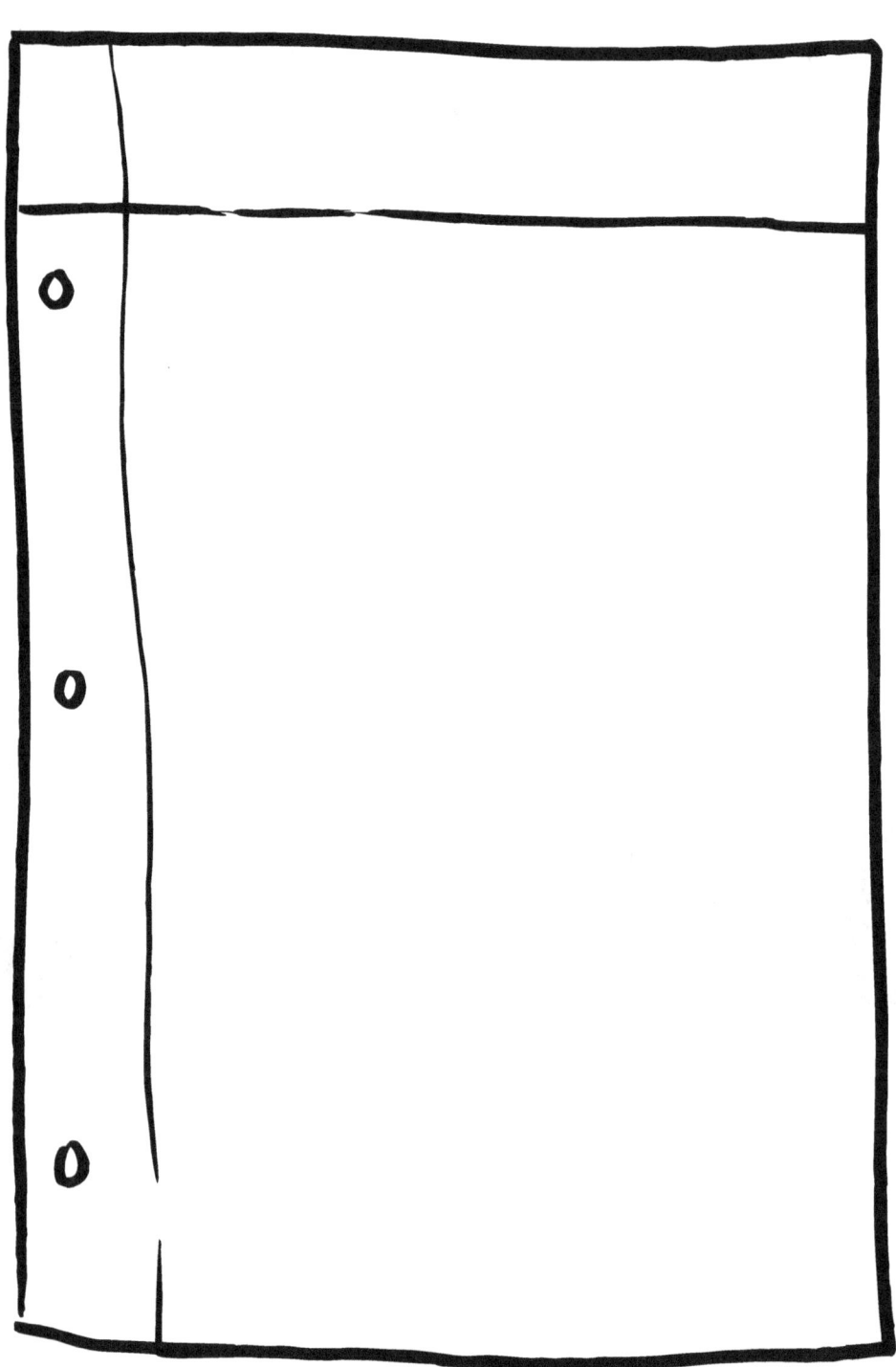

Bazooka Boys ★ Relationships

FAMILIES WHO STICK TOGETHER STAY STRONG

(20 minutes)

Supplies

- Popsicle sticks
- Wood glue

What Should We Do Next?

1. Glue five sticks together in a stack with the wood glue. Let dry for at least 30 minutes.

2. Once the glue has dried, hold the stack of sticks in your hand. Then think of something you could not do without the support of your family.

3. Now, break the individual stick. This stick should break easily. Now, try to break the stack of glued sticks.

4. Families need to stick together to stay strong. God has designed families to be stronger together than apart!

Bazooka Boys ★ Relationships

ELDERS

WHAT'S THE POINT?

God has placed people in authority over our lives and we need to treat them with honor and respect.

THEME VERSE

*For all **authority** comes from God, and those in positions of authority have been placed there by God.*
—Romans 13:1

RELATED BIBLE STORY

Jesus on Authority
Matthew 22:15–22

We've talked a lot about the relationships God brings into our lives to help us. We've talked about friends who come alongside us and are our companions on our journey. We've talked about our families, who stand by us and help take care of us. But today we are going to talk about one more group of people God brings into our worlds to teach us. They're called "elders."

Elder is kind of a funny, old fashioned word that we don't use very much, but let me tell you who your elders are. An elder is anyone older than you, anyone who is in leadership over you, or anyone who has any kind of authority in your life. Let's take a closer look at each of those three areas and see who the elders in your life are.

First of all, an elder is

 ## 1. SOMEONE OLDER THAN YOU.

Can you think of someone in your life who is older than you? Yes, your friend down the street may be two months older than you, but that doesn't necessarily make him your elder. What I'm talking about is someone who is a few years older than you or an adult. It could be a parent, grandparent, aunt and uncle, teacher, or simply someone walking on the street who's older than you. Those people are your elders because they were born before you.

Bazooka Boys ★ Relationships

WEEK 4

We're supposed to honor people who are older than we are. They have experienced lots of things in their lives that we haven't experienced yet, and God wants us to honor them with our words, actions, and attitudes. When we honor them, we're recognizing that they know things we don't know and that we respect their position.

Colton was getting on a bus at the airport to go on vacation with his family. The bus was really crowded and there were only a few more seats available. He had just settled into his seat when a woman who looked about the age of his grandmother walked onto the bus. There were no seats left, and the woman was left standing in the middle of the aisle. As soon as Colton's dad noticed the woman standing there, he jumped up and offered his seat to the older woman. She thanked him and quietly slipped into his father's seat.

After they got off the plane, Colton asked his dad a question: "Dad, why did you give that woman your seat on the bus?"

"Well," his dad replied, "it's a way to honor her because she is older than me. It was something I could do to show her respect."

There are lots of ways you can honor the older people in your life. Colton's Dad showed us a **HUGE** way—doing kind things for people older than you are. Offering them your seat, opening a door for them, helping them carry something to their car,...these are all ways you can show respect for someone older than you.

Another way you can honor your elders is by being kind and nice to people who are older. Sometimes younger people don't really appreciate people who are older than them. They can ignore them or sometimes even make fun of them, but that's not the kind of attitude God wants you to have toward people older than you. God wants you to honor and respect the elders in your life because they've gone before you and have wisdom and experiences you can learn from!

1 Peter 5:5 says, *"In the same way, you younger men must accept the authority of the elders. And all of you, serve each other in humility, for God opposes the proud but favors the humble."* God wants you to have a humble, serving heart toward the older people in your life. This attitude pleases God, and He will bless you for your kindness toward your elders.

The second group of people who are your elders are

2. THOSE WHO ARE IN LEADERSHIP OVER YOU.

Zeke was really excited to join the book club at his local library. He was looking forward to discussing all his favorite books and spending time with other boys who loved to read as much as he did.

The first day of book club came and he met Blake, who was the leader of the group. Blake was only a couple years older than Zeke, but the Librarian had put him in charge of the group. Zeke instantly knew that Blake was going to get on his nerves. He was kind of a know-it-all and never really gave the other people in the group a chance to talk. He was also pretty bossy and set up a whole lot of rules and guidelines for how the book club was going to run.

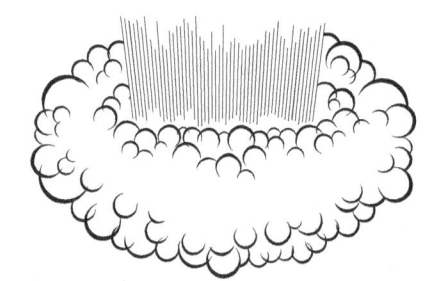

Every time Zeke went to the library for book club, he would start to get frustrated. He thought to himself, "I could do a way better job leading the group than Blake is." He would think negatively about Blake and his dumb rules and super smarty pants attitude.

One day Zeke decided to talk to his mom about the book club situation. He explained his frustrations and waited for his mother's advice.

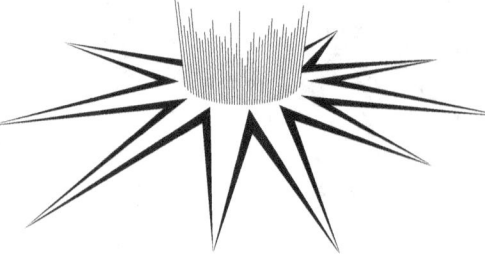

Bazooka Boys ★ Relationships

His Mom listened closely and then took a deep breath and gave Zeke some important advice:

"I know that sometimes it's difficult to be in a group where the leader does things differently than you would do them. I've been in that same position many times. But, as long as you're part of the group, you need to honor Blake's leadership. You can do that by trying to keep a good attitude, trying to follow the rules and guidelines he set up, and by keeping your words and actions kind, even when you're frustrated."

"In the same way, you younger men must accept the authority of the elders. And all of you, serve each other in humility, for God opposes the proud but favors the humble."
–1 PETER 5:5

This wasn't exactly the answer that Zeke was hoping for. He wanted his Mom to say that if Blake was bugging him so much, then he should just quit the group or tell him he didn't like the way he was doing things. But his Mom was trying to teach him a very important lesson: it's important to honor people in leadership over us, even if we don't always like or agree with the way they're leading.

You see, the Bible tells us that **ANYONE** who is in **ANY** position of leadership over us has been put there by God. **SERIOUSLY!** Anyone who is a teacher, leader, mentor, or in some other position of leadership in your life has been put there by God because He wants you to learn something from them. Sometimes we can forget that, especially if we're frustrated with our teacher, small group leader, student council president, or anyone else who is a leader.

But God tells us how we should treat people who are in leadership over us. Romans 13:1 says, *"Everyone must submit to governing authorities. For all authority comes from God, and those in positions of authority have been placed there by God."* God has put them there, so our attitude should be respectful.

When you honor the leaders in your life, you're really saying, "God, I trust that you put this person in my life to teach me something." Perhaps God has given you a leader who will show you how to be kind and treat people well. Maybe God has given you a leader who can teach you special knowledge and insight. Or maybe they have a specific skill or talent they can help you grow or develop in your own life.

Sometimes, God allows us to be under a leader who simply shows us the way **NOT** to do things. No matter what, our response to people in leadership should be one of respect.

Zeke decided to be the best book club member he could possibly be, even though it was really hard sometimes. He decided to honor the commitment he made to be in the group and not quit. He respectfully followed the rules Blake set up, and when he made suggestions about how to make the group better, he did so with a respectful and humble attitude.

When the year ended, the librarian called him up and asked him if **HE** would be interested in leading the group for the next year. Hmm…very interesting!

You know what? Zeke was very excited to lead the group, and he knew **EXACTLY** the way he was going to do it. He knew he wanted to give the other kids plenty of time to share their opinions because he knew how frustrating it was when Blake dominated the conversation. He knew he wanted guidelines, but he approached the rules of the club differently than Blake did because of his own experiences.

Zeke realized God had rewarded his decision to honor the leader He had put over him. He realized there were a lot of things he had learned from Blake that were really helpful when it came time for **HIM** to lead the group. And he was especially thankful that he had been respectful of Blake when he was in charge, because this was the kind of attitude he wanted the members of his group to have toward him now. (Remember our super-secret special weapon? Treat others the way you want to be treated!)

KA-BOOM!!!

Bazooka Boys ★ Relationships

God will put hundreds of people in leadership over you during your lifetime. You can make a decision right now to be respectful, honoring, and to have a good attitude toward all the people in leadership over you.

So, God wants us to honor people older than us, people in leadership over us, and lastly, God wants us to honor

 ## 3. PEOPLE IN AUTHORITY OVER US.

Who is an authority in your life? Basically, it's anyone who has the power to get you into trouble. Your parents are your authority. Your teachers and principals are your authority. Your grandparents and aunts and uncles are your authority. The policemen in your town are your authority. Even the president is in authority over you!

1 Peter 2:13–14 tells us, *"For the Lord's sake, respect all human authority—whether the king as head of state, or the officials he has appointed."* God puts people in positions of authority in our families, communities, cities, and even our country. They're in the positions they're in because God has placed them there for a specific plan and purpose.

We are supposed to respect those people by honoring them with our attitude, speaking respectfully about them with our words, and by obeying the rules they put over us.

Sometimes we don't agree with everything the people in authority over us think or believe, but God still wants us to respect and honor them. It can be really easy to get frustrated and disappointed with the way some leaders behave, but God tells us we should pray for them and maintain a respectful attitude—even in our disagreement with them.

Jesus was actually caught in a situation where some people were trying to get Him to say something bad about the people in authority over Him. When Jesus was teaching on earth, the people in charge of the government were the Romans, and they were led by a man named Caesar. They were not leaders who honored God. Actually, they kind of looked at their country as a god. They wanted people to worship them and didn't like it when the people served God.

There were also some religious leaders who didn't like Jesus. They were trying to find ways to get Him in trouble and make Him look bad in front of other people. So, one day, they asked Him a question in front of the crowds.

Matthew 22:15–22 says, "*Then the Pharisees met together to plot how to trap Jesus into saying something for which He could be arrested. They sent some of their disciples, along with the supporters of Herod, to meet with Him.*

"*'Teacher,' they said, 'We know how honest You are. You teach the way of God truthfully. You are impartial and don't play favorites. Now tell us what You think about this: Is it right to pay taxes to Caesar or not?'*

"*But Jesus knew their evil motives. 'You hypocrites!' He said. 'Why are you trying to trap Me? Here, show Me the coin used for the tax.'*

"*When they handed Him a Roman coin, He asked, 'Whose picture and title are stamped on it?'*

"*'Caesar's,' they replied.*

"*'Well, then,' He said, 'give to Caesar what belongs to Caesar, and give to God what belongs to God.'*

"*His reply amazed them, and they went away.*"

You see, the religious leaders were hoping to get Jesus to say something bad about the government and people in authority over the area where He was living. But Jesus refused to do it. He chose to honor the authority God had placed over Him, even though He didn't like **A LOT** of the things they were saying and doing. He recognized the importance of honoring the authority God had place in leadership at the time.

Bazooka Boys ★ Relationships

You can honor those in authority in your life by speaking respectfully about them. You can honor the authority in your life by following the rules and laws of the land. And you can especially honor authority by praying for them and doing everything you can to be a godly influence and example to all the people you come into contact with.

God wants you to be respectful of your elders. It pleases His heart when you honor those in leadership over you. You know why? 'Cause when you respect the elders in your life, you're really respecting God. You're acknowledging that He's in charge of everything and that you trust He is putting you right where you need to be. You're trusting His plan for your life. You're saying you believe He's in control, even if you don't always understand how or why He's doing the things He's doing.

Honor the authority in your life. Sometimes it's hard, but God will help you have the right attitude. He will help you be a good example to others of what it means to live a life that belongs to Jesus.

Closing Prayer: *Dear God, I want to honor You by honoring the elders in my life. Help me to treat the older people in my life with dignity and respect. Show me how I can support and learn from people You have put in leadership over my life. And I pray for the people in authority in my school, city, and country. I pray You would give them wisdom and teach me how to have a respectful and helpful attitude toward them. I love You, Jesus. Amen.*

ACTIVITY SHEET

WEEK 4

God wants you to be respectful of your elders. It pleases His heart when you honor those in leadership over you.

What are some ways you can respect the people in authority over you?

Solve each puzzle by substituting the letters for the numbers.

1	2	3	4	5	6	7	8
D	K	A	N	R	E	Y	I

9	10	11	12
B	P	I	O

Key

1. __P__ __R__ __A__ __Y__
    10   5   3   7

2. __O__ __B__ __E__ __Y__
    12   9   6   7

3. __B__ __E__
    9   6

   __K__ __I__ __N__ __D__
    2   11   4   1

"For all authority comes from God, and those in positions of authority have been placed there by God." (Romans 13:1, NLT)

What are some ways you can honor the leaders in your life?

Unscramble the words to find your answer.

Scrambled Words:	Write your answers here:
1. iseltn	
2. oyeb	
3. rpay	
4. eahv a dgoo tdetutai	

Scripture Puzzle

Step 1: Solve the Scripture Puzzle

Unscramble each of the clue words to solve the following statement:

An elder is anyone _____ than you, anyone who is in

_____ over you, or anyone who has any kind of

_____ in your life.

Clue Words:

ERDOL __ __ __ __ __
        15 14 22 1 17

RILPEAHESD __ __ __ __ __ __ __ __ __ __
           23 2 20 24 6 19 8 12 13 21

TORYUHAIT __ __ __ __ __ __ __ __ __
          18 7 9 16 5 3 10 11 4

Answers: Older, Leadership, Authority

Bazooka Boys ★ Relationships

Step 2: Copy the letters in the numbered cells above to the cells below with the same number to discover another scripture regarding authority.

```
__ V __ __ __ N __ / M __ __ __ / __ __ B M __ __
 1   2  3  4  5  6    7  8  9    8  7     10  9

__ __ M __ __ F / __ __ / __ __ __ /
12 13    8  6 23    9 15    9 16  2

G __ V __ __ N __ N G /
   5    1 17    10

__ __ __ __ __ __ __ __ __ __ , / F __ __ /
18  7  9 12  5 19 10  9 13  6  8         5  3

__ __ __ __ __ / __ __ / N __ /
 9 12  1 17  1   13  8       5

__ __ __ __ __ __ __ __ __ / __ X C __ __ __ /
20  7  9 16  5  3 13  9  4    1         1 21 11

__ __ __ __ / W __ __ C __ / G __ __ /
 9 12 20  9     12 13   12     5 22

__ __ __ / __ __ __ B __ __ __ __ __ __ /
12 18  8    2  8  9 18   23 10  8 12  1 24

__ __ __ / __ __ __ __ __ __ __ __ __ __ /
11 12  1   20  7  9 12  5 19 13  9 13  1  8

__ __ __ __ / __ X __ __ / __ __ V __ /
 9 12 18 11    2      13  8  9   12 18    1

B __ __ N / __ __ __ B __ __ __ __ __ __ /
   1  2      1  8 11 20  14 13  8 12  1 24

B __ / G __ __ . —Romans 13:1 NIV
   4      5 24
```

BAZOOKA BREAKDOWN

Today we learned that an elder is someone who is:

1. Someone who is _____ than you.

2. Someone who is in _____ over you.

3. Someone who is an _____ in your life.

Who are some of the people who are in leadership in your life?

It is so important to respect those in authority over you. Make a list of ways you can respect the elders God has put in your life.

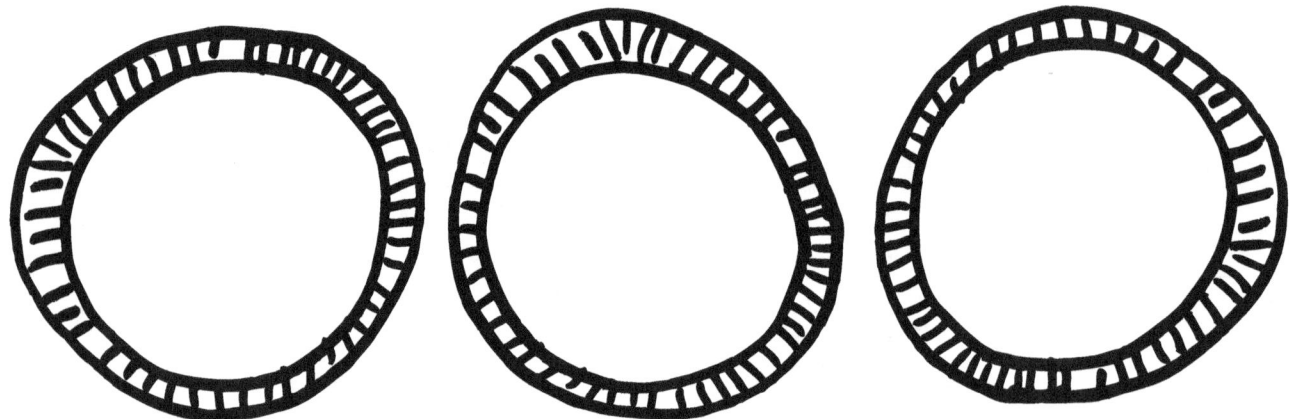

I CAN RESPECT MY ELDERS BY:

1. _____

2. _____

3. _____

4. _____

5. _____

Bazooka Boys ★ Relationships

Write out the theme verse three times and see if you can memorize it!

For all authority comes from God, and those in positions of authority have been placed there by God.
—Romans 13:1

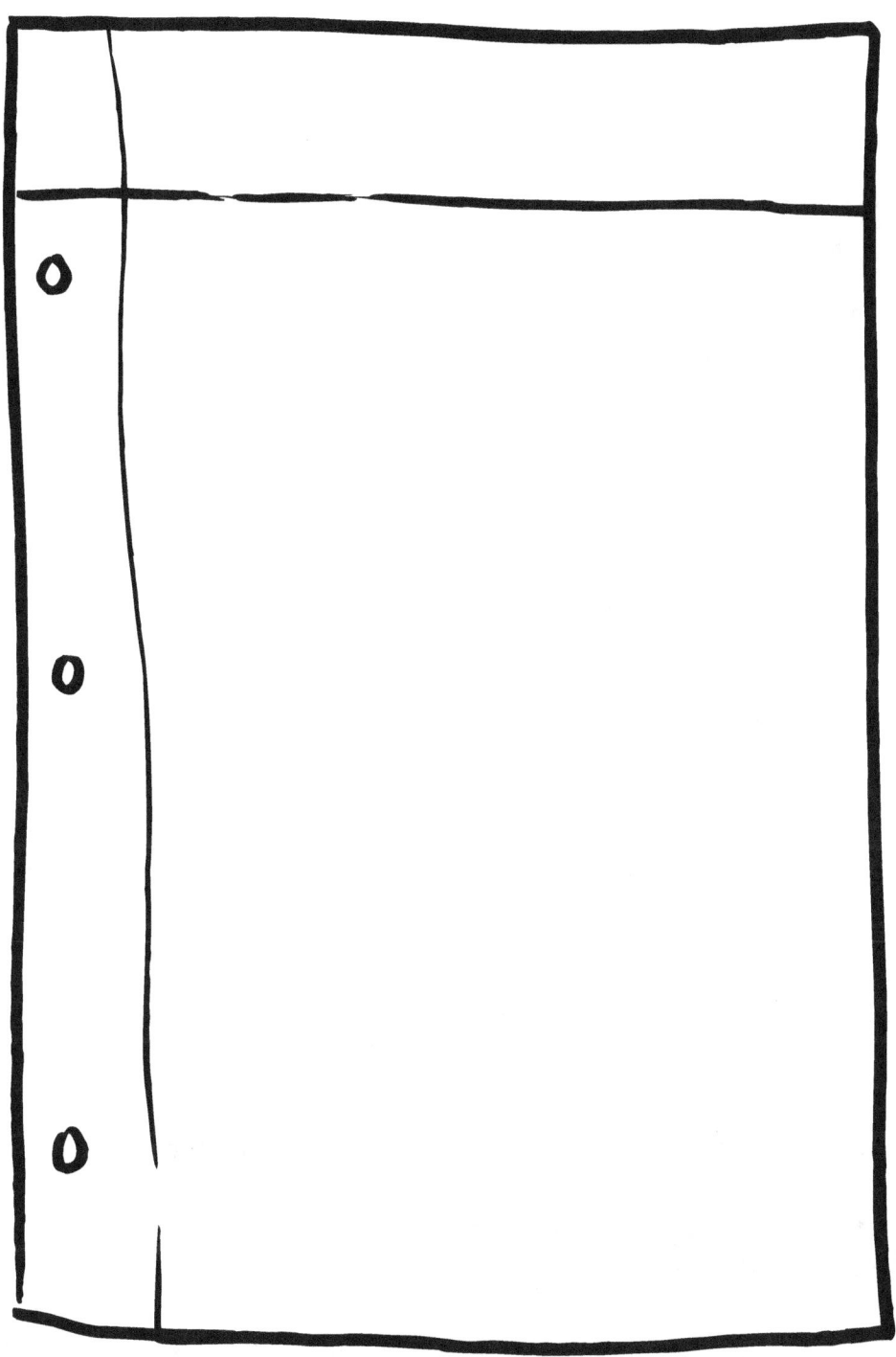

CANDY BAR AWARD

(20 minutes)

Supplies:

- 1.55 oz. Hershey bar
- Candy Bar Template
- Cardstock in a variety of colors
- Scissors
- Crayons/markers
- Double stick tape or glue stick

Prep:

- Copy template onto cardstock
- Trim excess paper around the template
- Purchase Hershey bars

What Should We Do:

1. Color and design the candy bar wrapper.

2. Write sentiments of thanks and appreciation on the wrapper.

3. Wrap the candy bar wrapper around the Hershey bar.

4. Use double stick tape or a glue stick to seal the wrapper around the back of the candy bar.

5. You can keep the original wrapper or take it off the bar.

6. Give to a grandparent, teacher, or leader to show them how much they're appreciated!

Bazooka Boys ★ Relationships

THANK YOU!!!

CANDY BAR

Nutrition Facts
Serving Size:
1 Good Elder
Romans 13:1 NLT

Amount / Serving	%DV
Appreciation	100%
Honor	100%
Respect	100%
Trust	100%
Happiness	100%

NET WT 1.55 oz

THANK YOU!!!

CANDY BAR

Nutrition Facts
Serving Size:
1 Good Elder
Romans 13:1 NLT

Amount / Serving	%DV
Appreciation	100%
Honor	100%
Respect	100%
Trust	100%
Happiness	100%

NET WT 1.55 oz

THINGS CHANGE

WHAT'S THE POINT?
Everything in the world changes, but God will **NEVER** change.

THEME VERSE
I am the Lord, and I do not change.
—Malachi 3:6

RELATED BIBLE STORY
The Many Changes in the Life of Joseph
Genesis 39

What's your favorite season? I **LOVE** fall. I love it when the leaves are turning different colors. I love it when the weather starts to turn cooler and you get to jump in piles of leaves. I even like it when the stores are filled with back to school supplies. I may not **LOVE** the idea that my kids are going back to school, but it sure is fun picking out new pencils and erasers and markers, right? Okay…you don't have to answer that question.

Those first days of school are crazy. Talk about changes! Just a few short weeks before school starts, you're swimming at the pool, sleeping in on summer vacation, and staying up late playing with your friends. But every year, no matter how much you try and pretend it isn't coming, the seasons change, summer ends, and fall begins.

But you know, not all change is fun. Sometimes change can be really hard. There are a lot of things in my life that have changed and sometimes I've had a really hard time adjusting to those changes.

CHANGE IS HARD.

Maybe you've had some things change in your life and you've had a hard time working through them. Maybe you have had to change schools and you're struggling to fit in at your new school and you're really missing your old friends.

Maybe your family has changed. Maybe you have a new brother or sister or maybe things have changed between your parents and you've had to adjust to **BIG** changes at home.

Bazooka Boys ★ Relationships

Maybe your friends are changing. Maybe you had a friend move away. Or maybe the boys you used to be really close to just aren't that close any more. Maybe they're starting to be interested in things you aren't interested in and you find yourselves drifting apart.

Maybe you're dealing with a sickness or something with your health that makes you unable to do things like you used to do, and so you have to change the way you spend your time.

Or maybe **YOU** are changing. You're getting older. You don't feel the same way you used to and you kind of feel like your whole life is upside down.

Change is hard. And change happens to everyone! Just when you think you have everything figured out, something happens and you have to start all over again. It can be really frustrating to have to deal with things changing all the time. It can make you feel sad, scared, discouraged, and lots of other things. It can make you feel like you're on shaky ground.

How many of you have ever been in a bouncy house? You know, those big things filled with air where you jump up and down? Or maybe you've been on a trampoline with a bunch of other people. Have you ever tried to walk through a bouncy house or walk on a trampoline when other people are jumping all around you?

You try to steady yourself and walk, but with every step the ground around you lifts and dips and moves. You try to shift your weight to keep your balance, but just when you think you have a steady place to stand, the ground beneath you moves again and you fall on your butt!

Sometimes that's **EXACTLY** how it feels trying to walk through your life when everything around you is changing. You can feel like you can't quite get your footing. You can feel lost. You can feel shaky and insecure. You might be wondering what you can count on when you look at everything around you that keeps changing.

The truth is things change. Actually, everything in the whole entire world changes and will continue to change except one thing. Do you know what that is?

GOD.

God never changes. He's always the same. Always. Forever. You can count on it.

No matter how many things in your life are changing, He is always the same.

"I am the Lord, and I do not change."—Malachi 3:6

God will never, ever change. He is exactly the same today as He has always been. That can be hard for us to understand because everything around us changes. But the truth is that God will remain **EXACTLY** the same, no matter what.

Hebrews 13:8 says, that *"Jesus Christ is the same yesterday, today, and forever."* He will **NEVER, EVER** change.

We can lean on God to help us with whatever changes we are going through!

Imagine that you're back in that bouncy house with everything moving and shaking when suddenly you see a handle along the edge of the wall. You grab onto it and suddenly, even though everything around you is moving, you're able to keep your balance because you're holding onto the handle.

Or imagine that you are on that bouncy-wouncy trampoline. And suddenly a friend who's standing along the edge reaches out a hand to you. As you walk forward, the ground beneath you is still moving like crazy, but you're not falling because you have something steady to hold onto.

You know what? When you're going through changes in your life and you feel like everything is topsy-turvy, **GOD** will be like that handle that you can grab on to so you can stay steady. When everything around you feels like it's on shaky ground, **GOD** will be that hand that reaches out and gives you something strong and stable to keep you from falling.

Bazooka Boys ★ Relationships

He will be something you can keep your eyes on while everything else is going crazy around you. He will be something that will keep you steady when you don't know who or what you can count on. When everything around you is changing, and you don't know what to do, **GOD** will remain steady and sure.

So, how do we get through all the changes in our lives? What do we do when things around us are changing and we don't know what to do?

 ## 1. REMEMBER THAT CHANGE IS HARD.

Can I tell you something? It's okay to be sad about the things that are changing in your world. It's okay to feel upset that your friend doesn't live here anymore. It's okay to be nervous going to a new school or a new church. It's okay to be upset that your parents are having problems. It's really important to be honest about how you're feeling.

Have you ever just been in a really **BAD** mood? You're just cranky and upset and you don't really know why? Sometimes I get that way and the best thing I know to do in those moments is to just sit down and ask myself, "What am I upset about?"

Once I do that, I usually feel a lot better and can start to deal with whatever situation is bothering me instead of just sitting there being a crabby pants.

> "I AM THE LORD, AND I DO NOT CHANGE."
> —Malachi 3:6

It's important to admit to yourself that you're having a hard time with the changes in your life. And more important than that —it's so good to go to Jesus and tell Him about the things that are bothering you. He already knows—because He knows everything about you! But when we go to Him and talk to Him and ask Him to help us deal with the changes in our lives, something really cool happens.

First of all, He will help us! He will give us creative ideas for dealing with the situation. He will give us patience and peace to face anything that comes our way.

And He will also comfort us! This means that when you're feeling sad or upset, God will help you feel better. He will remind you how much He loves you and that He's always got your back. That sure makes me feel better!

The second way you can deal with change in your life is to

2. REMEMBER THAT GOD IS WITH YOU.

There's a story in the Bible about a guy who went through a **WHOLE** lot of changes. His name was Joseph.

Joseph had twelve brothers. When he was 17 years old, he told his dad some of the bad things that his brothers were doing and after that, they did NOT like him at all! So one day, they threw him into a big pit and then they sold him as a slave to some people from Egypt.

Yikes! Those were some **PRETTY** big changes for Joseph. His family fell apart and his brothers **SOLD** him! He had to go to a new country where He didn't know anyone. Can you imagine how hard that would have been?

Joseph's life was on pretty shaky ground! But no matter what he faced or how crazy things got, God was with Joseph. When He was sad, God was there. When He was scared, God was there. When He was lonely, God was there. When He had no idea what to do, God was there.

And God will be there for you too!

Bazooka Boys ★ Relationships

Hebrews 13:5 says, *"Since God assured us, "I'll never let you down, never walk off and leave you."* (MSG)

When **YOU** are sad, God will be there. When **YOU** are scared, God will be there. When **YOU** are lonely, God will be there. When **YOU** have no idea what to do, God will be there.

Always. Forever. No exceptions. He's not going anywhere. You can be **SURE** He will always be with you—no matter what.

And the last way you deal with change in your life is to:

 **3. LOOK AHEAD.**

The hardest thing about change is that you MISS the way things were before! You think back to the way things used to be and you can't imagine things being as good as that ever again.

You wonder if you'll ever have friends as awesome as the ones you had before. You wonder if you'll ever feel happy with your family with all the new changes. You wonder if you'll ever like your new school. You wonder if you'll ever feel confident about yourself again.

But you know what? God has great things **AHEAD** for you!

You might not be able to see it right now. You might not be able to figure out how it's going to all work out. You might not even feel like it. **BUT GOD** has great things ahead for you!

1 Peter 1:6 says, *"So be truly glad. There is wonderful joy ahead, even though you have to endure many trials for a little while."* Things might be hard for a little while when you are dealing with changes, but there is wonderful **JOY** ahead of you.

The best way to get through a change is to keep your eyes on what's ahead.

Philippians 3:13 says, *"Brothers and sisters, I myself don't think I've reached it, but I do this one thing: I forget about the things behind me and reach out for the things ahead of me."* (CEB)

Now, to forget what is behind—does that mean that we can't still love our old friends? Does it mean we can't remember how great those old times were? Does it mean you can't wish your family would be the way it used to be?

What is **DOES** mean is that you can't stop living your life and get **STUCK** where you are because you won't look ahead to what God has for you. You can remember and love **ALL** the things that used to be **AND** still reach out for all the new things God has planned for you.

God has **GREAT** things ahead of you! He has new friends for you to meet. He has new things He wants you to do. He has plans to help you deal with your new family situation. He has new things for you to learn. He has new places for you to make a difference. And great big exciting things for every area of your life.

And **HE** is going to **BE THERE** for each and every one of them. James 1:17 says, *"Every good gift, every perfect gift, comes from above. These gifts come down from the Father, the creator of the heavenly lights, in whose character there is no change at all."* (CEB)

You can look forward to what God has for you because you **KNOW** He's going to be there. Hebrews 1:10–11 says, *"Earth and sky will wear out, but not You; they become threadbare like an old coat; You'll fold them up like a worn-out cloak, and lay them away on the shelf. But You'll stay the same, year after year; You'll never fade, You'll never wear out."* (MSG)

Bazooka Boys ★ Relationships

Everything changes. People change. Circumstances change. Families Change. Jobs and schools change.

BUT GOD NEVER, EVER CHANGES.

Closing Prayer: *Dear God, there are a lot of things changing in my life. I need You to help me work through these things in my life. Help me to know You are with me and to trust that You have great things in store for my future. I love you. Amen.*

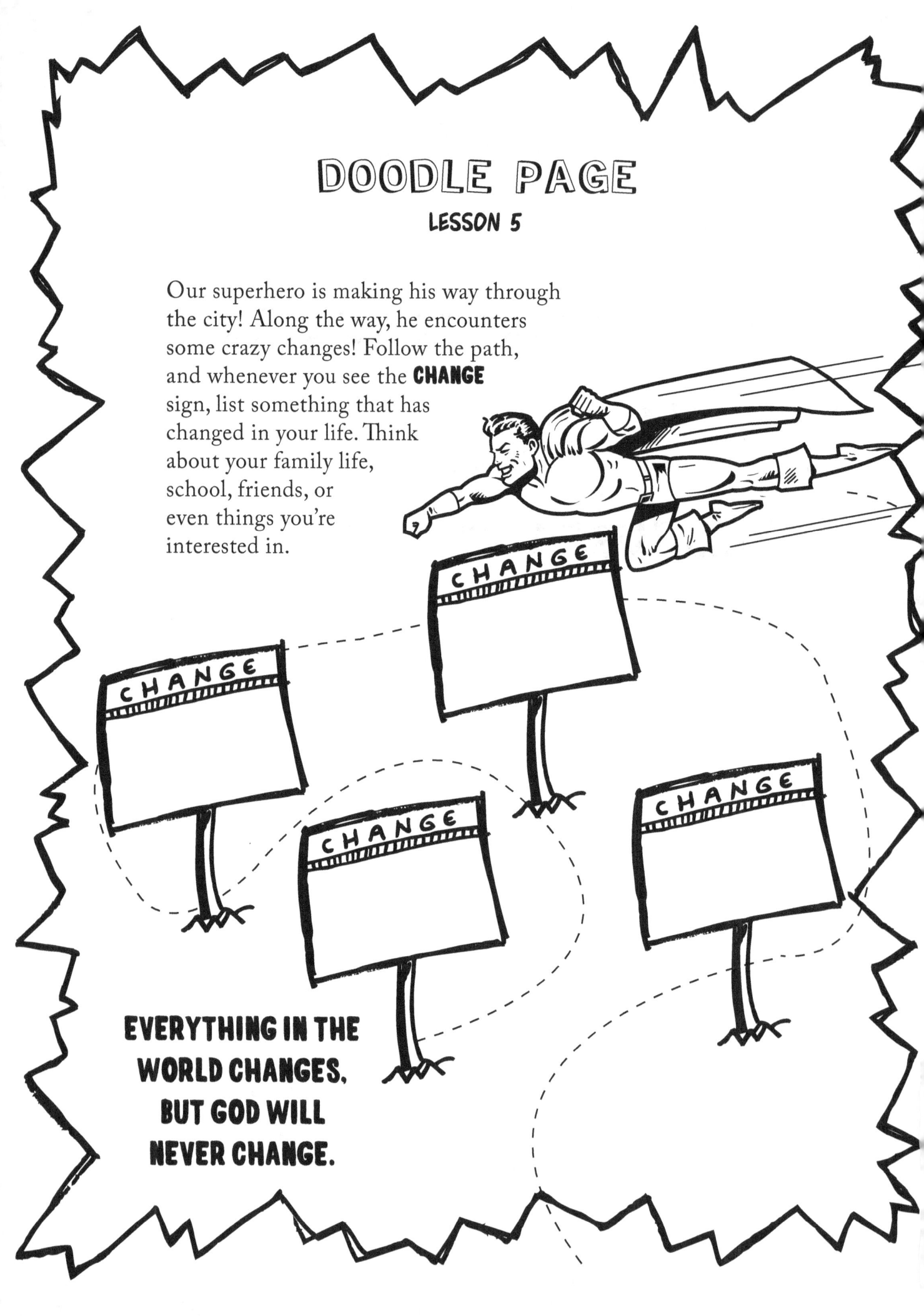

ACTIVITY SHEET

List 5 things that have changed in your life over the last year.

1.

2.

3.

4.

5.

List 5 new things God has ahead for you.

1.

2.

3.

4.

5.

Look up the following verses in your Bible and fill in the blanks (all Scripture NIV).

"*I the LORD do not _____.*" (Malachi 3:6)

"*Jesus Christ is the _____ yesterday and today and forever.*" (Hebrews 13:8)

"*But You remain the _____, and Your years will never end.*" (Psalm 102:27)

"*Every good and perfect gift is from above, coming down from the Father of the heavenly lights, who does not _____ like shifting shadows.*" (James 1:17)

"*Brothers, I do not consider myself yet to have taken hold of it. But one thing I do: Forgetting what is _____ and straining toward what is _____.*" (Philippians 3:13)

"*In this you greatly _____, though now for a little while you may have had to suffer grief in all kinds of trials.*" (1 Peter 1:6)

"*Keep your lives free from the love of money and be _____ with what you have, because God has said, "Never will I _____ you; never will I _____ you.*" (Hebrews 13:5)

BAZOOKA BREAKDOWN

It's important to remember that no matter what changes are going on in your life, that God will always be with you. How does that make you feel when you know God will never leave your side?

"I AM THE LORD, AND I DO NOT CHANGE."

—MALACHI 3:6

WEEK 5

Read the story of Joseph found in Genesis 39 listed below. Circle or highlight every time to read the words, "The Lord was with Joseph."

Vs 1-4: When Joseph was taken to Egypt by the Ishmaelite traders; he was purchased by Potiphar, an Egyptian officer. Potiphar was captain of the guard for Pharaoh, the king of Egypt.

The Lord was with Joseph, so he succeeded in everything he did as he served in the home of his Egyptian master. Potiphar noticed this and realized that the Lord was with Joseph.

Then Potiphar's wife made up an awful story about Joseph and told her husband a big lie.

Vs 19-23: Potiphar was furious when he heard his wife's story about how Joseph had treated her. So he took Joseph and threw him into the prison where the king's prisoners were held, and there he remained. But the Lord was with Joseph in the prison and showed him his faithful love. And the Lord made Joseph a favorite with the prison warden. Before long, the warden put Joseph in charge of all the other prisoners and over everything that happened in the prison. The warden had no more worries, because Joseph took care of everything. The Lord was with him and caused everything he did to succeed.

Bazooka Boys ★ Relationships

Write out the theme verse three times and try to memorize it!

I am the Lord, and I do not change."
—Malachi 3:6

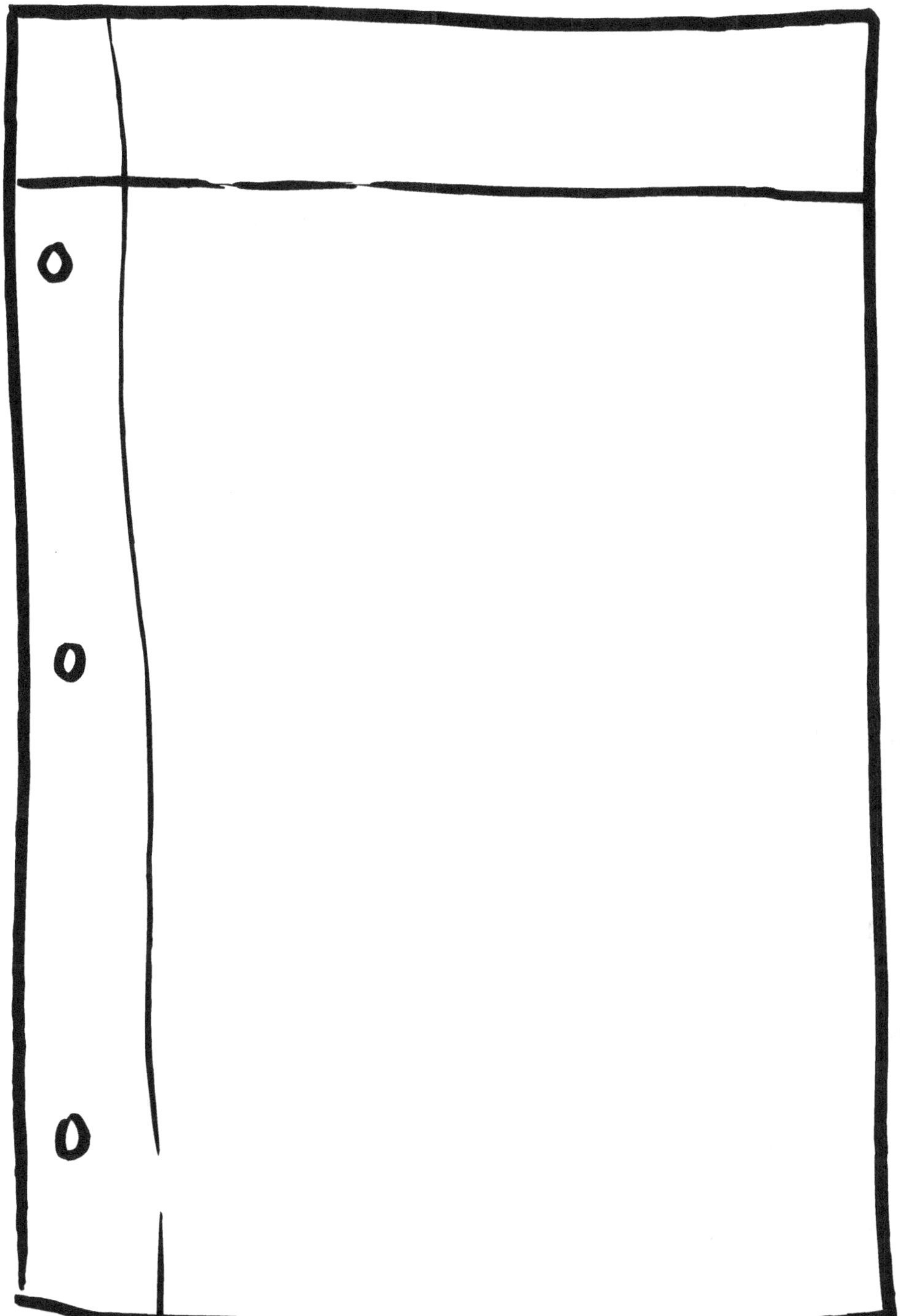

GOD IS MY ROCK CHOKER

(20 minutes)

Supplies:

- One small rock
- Plain silver 22 gauge wire (approximately 15 inches)
- Scissors
- Pencil
- Needle-nose pliers
- Cord or leather thread
- Fine point permanent black marker

Prep:

- With the black marker, write Malachi 3:6 on the rock.
- Cut floral wire into 15 inch length.
- Cut cord or thread into necklace length.

What Should We Do Next:

1. Place the rock at the center of a 15-inch long piece of wire.
2. Wrap the wire around the rock a few times to secure it.
3. Twist together the ends, and then wrap the twist around a pencil to form a loop.
4. Use needle nose pliers to close the loop, and then cut off the excess wire with a scissors.
5. To finish, thread a necklace-length piece of cord or leather through the loop and knot the ends.

Bazooka Boys ★ Relationships

WATCH YOUR WORDS

WHAT'S THE POINT?
God wants us to choose to use kind and encouraging words.

THEME VERSE

Words kill, words give life; they're either poison or fruit —you choose.
—Proverbs 18:21 (MSG)

RELATED BIBLE STORY

Taming the Tongue
James 3:5–12

Have you ever had someone say something really, really nice about you? Maybe your mom told everyone in your family something really special about you. Or maybe a teacher pointed out how much she appreciated your help in class. Or maybe a friend thanked you for hanging out with him.

There's nothing quite as awesome as someone saying something nice to you. Something inside of you just feels **SO** good when someone speaks kind words to you. You feel happy, confident, and proud of yourself. I love it when people say nice things about me!

Now, let me ask you **tHIS** question. Have you ever had someone say something "not so nice" about you? Yup… me too. Maybe a friend got mad at you and said some things about you behind your back. Or maybe a teacher said something that really bugged you. Or maybe your brother or sister called you a name.

There's nothing quite as **AWFUL** as having someone say something bad about you. You get a horrible feeling in your stomach and you just want to find a place to hide out. You feel sad, nervous, and alone. I **HAtE** it when people say bad things about me!

ISN't It CRAZY tO SEE HOW POWERFUL OUR WORDS ARE?

A kind word from someone can make you feel **AMAZING**, and an unkind word can make you feel **HORRIBLE**. I think it's amazing how something as little as a **WORD** can have so much power over how we feel.

The Bible says, "*Words kill, words give life; they're either poison or fruit—you choose.*" (Proverbs 18:21, MSG) What do you think that means? It means our words have the power to tear people down or build people up. And you and I have to choose what kind of words we're going to use.

Luke hated going to the bus stop. Every morning he would get on his coat and shoes and backpack and head for the front door and stop and say a prayer because he was **SO** nervous to walk outside to wait for the bus with the other kids.

Bazooka Boys ★ Relationships

He was so nervous because there were three boys at the bus stop who didn't say very nice things to him. Every morning, they made fun of him and called him names. Luke had **NO** idea why these boys were so mean to him, but it seemed like no matter what he did, they found something mean to say.

Their words were powerful. Even if Luke was having the best morning possible, once the boys at the bus stop finished with him, he always felt horrible. Their words hurt.

The Bible tells us that our words have the power to hurt, but they also have the power to build someone up. Our words can tear down, but our words also have the power to make us feel stronger and more confident too!

One day Luke got to the bus stop and was bracing himself for the boys to start bothering him. But before they could open their mouths, suddenly another boy spoke up. "Hey Luke, I heard you got that new super cool video game! You're so lucky! I bet you're already to level five 'cause you're so good at gaming." Luke was shocked! He replied quietly, "Um…yeah…it's pretty sweet. I got through level six last night." The other boy spoke again. "Well, if I ever get that game I'm totally gonna have you come get me through those levels. You're DA MAN!"

Luke could not believe it. He looked at the mean boys and their mouths were wide open. The nice things this boy said to him just shut those other boys right up. The power of those nice words was **WAY** stronger than the power of the negative ones.

I know that sometimes it can be hard to control the words that are coming from your mouth. There are times when I say things and then wonder, "Why in the world did I say that?" It can be easy to say mean things to someone when you're frustrated with them. It

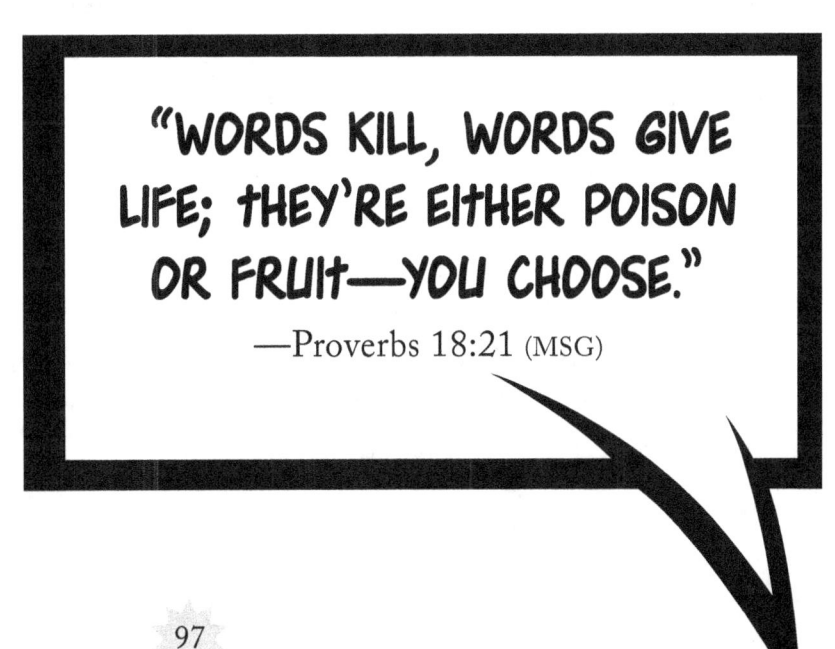

"WORDS KILL, WORDS GIVE LIFE; THEY'RE EITHER POISON OR FRUIT—YOU CHOOSE."
—Proverbs 18:21 (MSG)

can make you feel strong when you use the power of your words to tear someone else down. And you can feel important when you talk about another person.

But God is very clear in the Bible that He wants us to be very, very careful about the words we use. James 3:2 says, "*For if we could control our tongues, we would be perfect and could also control ourselves in every other way.*" God knows that if we control our tongues—or if we control the things we say—we'll be able to control ourselves in lots of different areas. Our words may be hard to control, but if we learn to be careful about the things we're saying, we'll be able to control LOTS of other things in our hearts!

Here are three ways we can choose to use the power of our words for GOOD and not EVIL.

Gossip is talking about other people behind their backs. It is sharing information or stories with other people. Most of the time, it's sharing things that are mean and hurtful, but it's even wrong to share information that isn't yours to share! Gossip is telling a story that can damage a person's reputation. It is talking or writing about another person or situation in order to turn another's opinion against that person or situation.

Sometimes we gossip because we're upset with a person and we don't know what to do about it, but the Bible says that if we have a problem with someone, we shouldn't talk to other people about it—we should go right to the person and talk it through with them! Matthew 18:15 (MSG) says, "*If a fellow believer hurts you, GO and tell him—work it out between the two of you.*"

Other times we gossip just because it seems fun. Sometimes we can talk about other people simply because we don't have anything better to talk about. Some people just think it's fun to say things about people's clothes or families or lots of other things. We can tell our friends a story that we may think is funny, but really, we're just making fun of someone else.

God does **NOT** want us to use other people that way. He cares about each and every person, and when we say things about other people, it makes God's heart sad. We should want to honor God by treating other people the way God wants us to treat them. Psalm 19:14 says, *"Let my words and my thoughts be pleasing to you, Lord."* (CEV)

God wants you to be a good friend. When you talk about other people behind their backs, you're not being a good friend.

Another way you can choose positive words is:

2. BE A TRUSTWORTHY FRIEND.

I had a friend who liked to talk about other people. He loved to tell what so-and-so did last weekend and who was fighting with whom. He loved to go through all the people we knew and point out all the things about them that he didn't like. He just **LOVED** to talk about other people.

I never felt comfortable when he talked about other people that way. But one day, something occurred to me that made me really re-think my friendship with him. I began to wonder—if he talked about **OTHER PEOPLE** all the time behind their backs, chances are he was talking about **ME** behind my back.

I have **ANOTHER** friend, who **NEVER** talks about other people. Anytime we are with other people and they start to say something about someone else, he either says something positive about that person or changes the subject. I really began to notice how hard he worked at not saying unkind things about people.

That friend made me realize two things. First of all, that I should be a lot more like him! I also realized I could always trust him. I never had to wonder if he was saying bad things

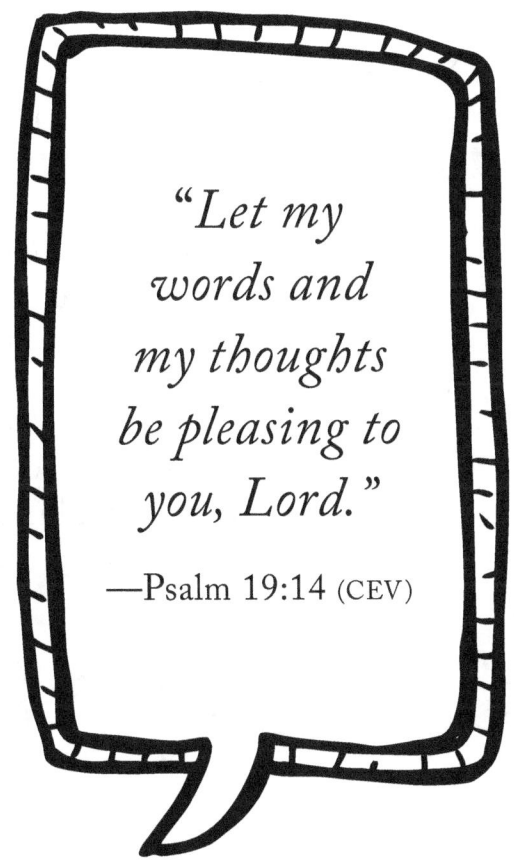

"Let my words and my thoughts be pleasing to you, Lord."

—Psalm 19:14 (CEV)

about me to other people. I could tell him anything and know that he wouldn't share it with anyone else.

I realized that the way this friend acted made me **TRUST** him. When you trust someone, it means that you feel safe with them. You don't wonder if they're **REALLY** your friend or not. You don't have to worry about them behaving one way when they're with you and another way when you're not around.

Not only should you try to fill your life with friends you can trust, you should **BECOME** a trustworthy friend! Make sure your friends know they can count on you to only use kind words about them. Show them your loyalty by refusing to talk about **ANYONE** behind their back. Proverbs 20:19 (CEB) says, "*A gossip tells secrets, so don't hang around with someone who talks too much.*"

The last way you can be a friend who chooses positive words is to:

 ## 3. ENCOURAGE OTHER PEOPLE.

We have talked about how powerful our words are. They can build people up, or they can tear them down. We can choose to use kind words or we can choose to use unkind words.

When you say kind words to people, you're encouraging them! When you point out the good things in people and tell them what you like about them, you're encouraging them! When you help people feel better about themselves, you're an encourager!

Each of us has a bucket! When someone says **KIND** words about you, they're filling up your bucket one little thing at a time. So maybe your

friend tells you he likes your jersey—he is filling your bucket! When your teacher tells you you did a good job—she's filling the bucket.

BUT when someone uses **UNKIND** words, they're actually taking things out of your bucket. Let's say someone tells you they don't like your new shoes—they're emptying your bucket. When you and your friend get in a fight and he says something mean to you—he's emptying your bucket.

So—do you think we should be friends who are emptying out buckets or filling them up? That's right! We should always find ways to **ENCOURAGE** and fill up the buckets of the people in our lives.

Ephesians 4:29 tell us, "*Let everything you say be good and helpful, so that your words will be an encouragement to those who hear them.*" Make a decision to be the kind of friend who always says good and helpful things. Be an encouraging friend.

Our words are powerful. We can choose to use our words to encourage and lift up our friends, or we can choose to use our words to tear them down. Let's be the kind of friends who make the right choice!

Closing Prayer: *Dear God, I thank You for the friends and family you have given me. Help me to not use words that tear down other people. Help me to not talk about people behind their backs. I want to be a trustworthy and encouraging friend. I love You, Jesus. Amen.*

DOODLE PAGE

LESSON 6

Our words and actions have the power to either build others up or tear them down. Think about some things in your life that have encouraged you and write those words next to the hearts. Then think of some things that have **NOT** been encouraging and write those near the skull and crossbones.

ACTIVITY SHEET

KINDERGARTEN AND 1ST GRADE

Each word or phrase has the power to encourage others or hurt others. Color the encouraging words and draw a line through the words that hurt.

"Words kill, words give life; they're either poison or fruit—you choose."
—Proverbs 18:21 (MSG)

YOU ARE AWESOME

THAT'S STUPID

YOU CAN DO IT!

I DON'T LIKE YOU

THANK YOU FOR BEING MY FRIEND

YOU CAN'T PLAY WITH ME

YOU ARE SO GOOD AT THAT!

I DON'T CARE WHAT YOU SAY

WAY TO GO!

I LOVE YOU

YOU ARE SO MEAN

I BELIEVE IN YOU

YOU DON'T FIT IN OUR GROUP

In the Bible, God is very clear that He wants us to be very, very careful about the words we use. Your words can build up those around you or tear them down.

Fill in the blanks below to start building up the friends and family in your life.

I can build up _____ with this word of encouragement:

I can build up _____ with this compliment:

I can build up _____ by thanking them for:

I can build up _____ by telling them this about God:

Each of us has a bucket! We want to feel encouraged, accepted, and loved. When someone uses **KIND** words about you, they're filling up your bucket one little thing at a time.

BUt when someone uses **UNKIND** words, they're taking things out of your bucket!

One week challenge! Reflect on the following questions, and at the end of each day, circle your answers. At the end of the week, fill in the blank.

1. Did I fill someone's bucket this week by being encouraging, kind, helpful, or thoughtful?

Monday	Yes	No
Tuesday	Yes	No
Wednesday	Yes	No
Thursday	Yes	No
Friday	Yes	No
Saturday	Yes	No
Sunday	Yes	No

If yes, how?_____

2. Did I say or do anything that might have emptied someone's bucket?

Monday	Yes	No
Tuesday	Yes	No
Wednesday	Yes	No
Thursday	Yes	No
Friday	Yes	No
Saturday	Yes	No
Sunday	Yes	No

If yes, how?_____

Did I apologize?   Yes   No

3. Is there anyone I know whose bucket is less than full and could really use a friend? Yes or No

If yes, who?_____

If yes, what could I do to help?_____

God wants us to choose to use kind and encouraging words.

The verses below talk about how we should watch our words. Read each verse in your Bible and fill in the missing word (all Scripture NIV).

1. James 3:2

We all stumble in many ways. If anyone is never at fault in what he says, he is a perfect man, able to keep his whole _____ in check.

2. Psalm 19:14

May the words of my mouth and the meditation of my _____ be pleasing in Your sight, O LORD, my Rock and my Redeemer.

3. Ephesians 4:29

Do not let any unwholesome talk come out of your _____, but only what is helpful for building others up according to their needs, that it may benefit those who _____.

4. Proverbs 20:19

A _____ betrays a confidence; so avoid a man who talks too much.

Bazooka Boys ★ Relationships

5. Matthew 18:15

If your brother _____ against you, go and show him his fault, just between the _____ of you. If he listens to you, you have won your brother over.

Word List

heart   two   body   listen   gossip   sins   mouth

BAZOOKA BREAKDOWN

Gossip is simply talking about other people behind their backs. One of our superheroes is gossiping. What should his friend say to him? Write your thoughts in the space below.

"Did you hear what Captain Thunder did yesterday?"

Bazooka Boys ★ Relationships

What are some ways you can be a trustworthy friend? Make a list of five things.

Write the theme verse three times and see if you can memorize it!

"Words kill, words give life; they're either poison or fruit—you choose."
—Proverbs 18:21 MSG

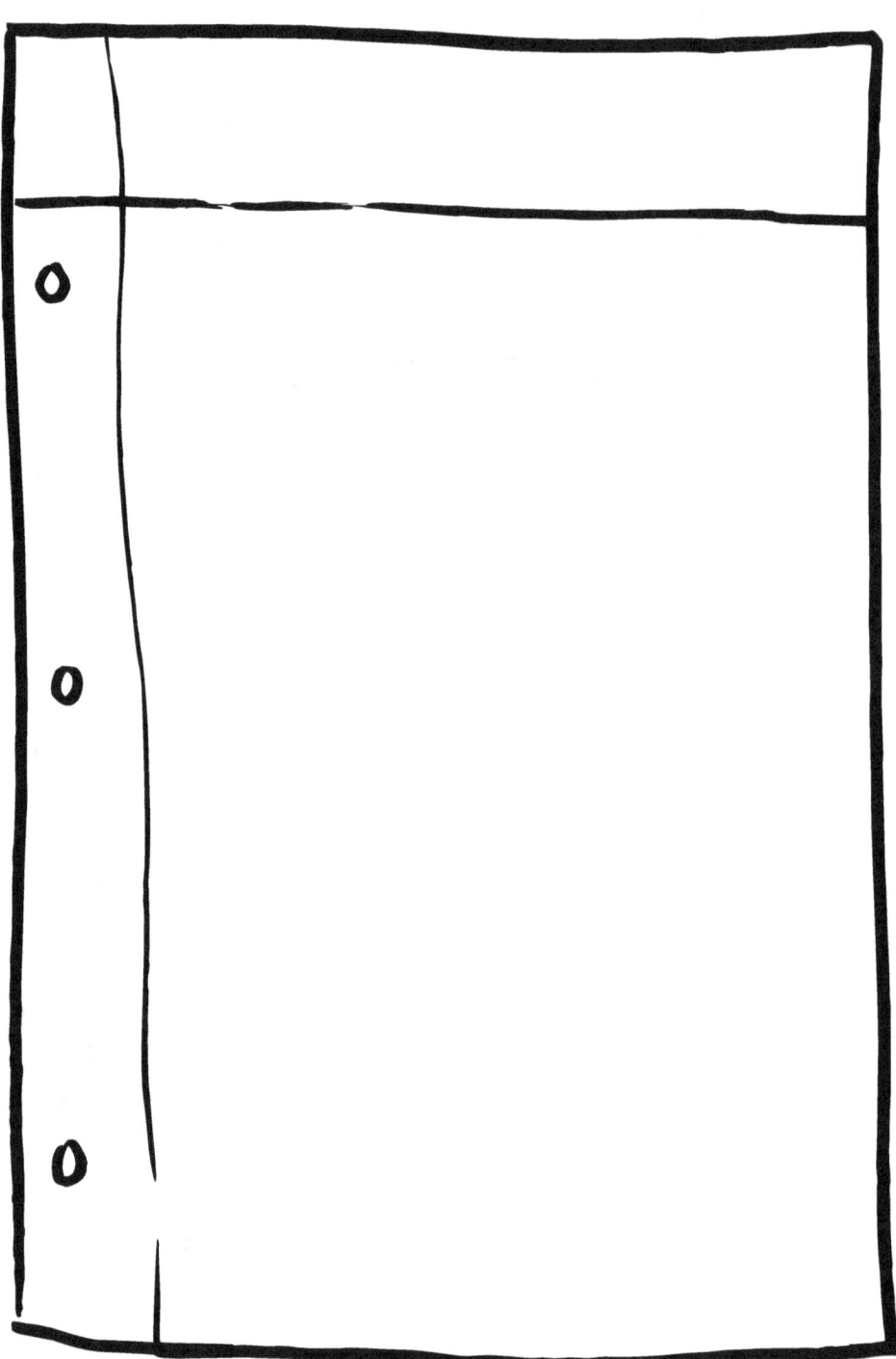

Bazooka Boys ★ Relationships

WEB OF WORDS SNACK

(20 minutes)

Supplies:

- Pretzel Sticks (6)
- White chocolate/bark candy coating
- Milk chocolate (baker's, candy coating, or chips)
- Raisins
- Baggie
- Wax paper
- Cookie sheet (optional)

What Should We Do Next?

1. Lay out pretzels in a "starburst" shape on the wax paper
2. Melt chocolate/bark coating
3. Place melted chocolate/bark coating in a plastic baggie
4. Cut the corner of the baggie (or use a pastry bag)
5. Place a dab of chocolate/bark in the middle of the pretzels
6. Then swirl the chocolate/bark around the pretzels creating your web
7. Place two raisins in the middle of the pretzels to create the spider body
8. Dab a small amount of melted chocolate/bark over the raisins
9. Place your webs in the refrigerator to set for at least 5 minutes

Bazooka Boys ★ Relationships

ATTENTION

WHAT'S THE POINT?
We should be known for the good things we do —not for stealing all the attention or doing negative things.

THEME VERSE
We were not looking for praise from you or anyone else.
—1 Thessalonians 2:6 (NIRV)

RELATED BIBLE STORY
Absalom
2 Samuel 14:25–2 Samuel 15:12

I L-O-V-E birthdays. I love everything about them. I love all the presents. I love the cake and candles. But mostly, it sure is fun to have a day where everyone points out how special you are. It's so nice to have people say nice things to you and give you gifts. It's fun to have a day where you are the center of attention.

Can you imagine if every day was your birthday? If everywhere you went, every day, people stopped you and handed you a gift? Or after every meal, your mom brought out a cake and everyone sang to you? That would be crazy…Crazy awesome!

Birthdays are fun because it's always nice to get attention. It feels good when people notice you and tell you you're awesome. Really, I think for most of us, it's important to feel like we matter to the people around us. We want to know that people love us and care about us. And on our birthdays, people take extra time to make sure we **KNOW** how important we are to them. It's really, really, nice!

But, what about all those other days? There are 364 days every year that are **NOT** your birthday. What do we do on those days when we aren't getting special attention? Some of you don't really like attention, so you're just fine on the non-birthday days! But for most of us, sometimes we need more attention than we're getting on those plain old everyday days.

Why does attention feel so good? Because we all want to know we're valuable! We want to know we're important to people. We want people to like us and we want to be winners. When someone gives you attention by saying something awesome about you, it makes you feel good about yourself. When someone gives you attention by asking you to do a special job, you feel great! When someone tells you you're amazing, you feel amazing!

There's nothing wrong with getting attention from other people. Actually, God loves it when we feel good about ourselves because He **LOVES** us. **HE** is your #1 fan. He loves every single tiny thing about you. So, when other people notice and value you, He likes it, too!

But sometimes, we can get the **WRONG** kind of attention. People can notice us because of the negative things we do. We can behave in a way that isn't kind

Bazooka Boys ★ Relationships

and loving and causes other people to notice us for the wrong reasons.

There was a boy in Michael's class who always seemed to have the teacher's attention, but Michael wasn't so sure it was the "good kind" of attention. This boy was always getting in trouble for being disrespectful. He would speak out of turn and say inappropriate things. The teacher spent a lot of time dealing with this boy's behavior. He sure was getting a lot of attention, but it wasn't for positive things.

Sometimes, we can get attention by doing or saying things that aren't honoring to God. Sometimes we can be bossy or rude or point out other people's weaknesses so we look stronger. God doesn't like it when we get that kind of attention. Sometimes we can get attention by telling a joke that has a bad word in it or makes fun of someone else. God doesn't want us to get attention like that, either.

Here are three things to remember when it comes to attention.

 ## 1. DON'T STEAL ALL THE ATTENTION.

Nick had a friend who **REALLY** loved to get attention. He loved to talk about the things HE was doing and point out the fact that he was the **BEST** player on the team and make sure everyone knew what **HE** wanted to do. He was super nice and really fun to be around, but it seemed like he always had to be the center of attention. After a while, his friends got tired of everything **ALWAYS** being about him. They got frustrated because he never seemed interested in listening to what **THEY** had to say. If the conversation wasn't focused on the things he wanted to talk about, he would stop listening.

God doesn't want us stealing all the attention! He doesn't want us to always make things about ourselves. **ACTUALLY**, the Bible says, "*Don't be selfish; don't try to impress others. Be humble, thinking of others as better than yourselves.*" (Philippians

2:3). When we're constantly demanding all the attention, we're really being selfish. We're not thinking of other people's feelings—we're just focusing on ourselves and what we want.

Good friends are interested in what other people have to say. Good friends like to point out the wonderful things in other people. Good friends don't steal all the attention.

Secondly, we need to remember:

 ## 2. DON'T TRY TO GET ATTENTION IN NEGATIVE WAYS.

It certainly is nice to have people pay attention to you, but sometimes you can start to want it so bad that you're willing to do anything to make people notice you. One way you can do that is by misbehaving just to get someone's attention. Sometimes that looks like acting out in school, disobeying your parents at home, and even fighting with your friends. You may be getting attention all right, but it's not for good things!

There's a guy in the Bible named Absalom who wanted attention **REALLY** badly. First of all, he was super obsessed with how he looked. He grew his hair so long that the Bible says it weighed **FIVE POUNDS**! That's a lot of hair. He was trying to get the attention of his father, King David, who was punishing him for some really bad behavior, so do you know what he did? He set **FIRE** to a field that belonged to one of the king's best friends! What in the world? That's a **CRAZY** way to try and get some attention!

"Don't be selfish; don't try to impress others. Be humble, thinking of others as better than yourselves."
—Philippians 2:3

But it didn't stop there. Absalom was so intent on getting the attention of people

that he began to plot and scheme about ways to take over the kingdom from his father. He made promises to people that he couldn't keep. He pretended to be friends with people just so he could get his own way. And eventually he sent secret messengers to all the people and stirred up rebellion against the king—his own father!

His need to be the best, to be the coolest, most admired, and powerful man eventually led to his death. As he was riding away from David's armies on his horse, his super long hair got caught in a tree and left him hanging there. The captain of David's army found him hanging there and plunged three daggers into his heart. Things did not end well for Absalom.

Don't try to get attention from things that aren't good. You're such an amazing kid—you don't need to do crazy stuff to make people notice you! Just be the awesome person God made you to be, and people will notice you for that!

And the last thing we need to remember is:

3. BE KNOWN FOR THE GOOD THINGS YOU DO FOR OTHER PEOPLE.

It would be cool if you were known as the best player on your baseball team. It would be awesome if you were known for being the fastest runner or a legendary gamer. You could be the funniest joke teller, the most amazing speller, or the person who can shove the most quarters up your nose (Note: You should **NEVER** shove quarters up your nose. Bad things could happen…very bad things…) Being known for any of those things would be pretty cool.

But what if you were known for something greater than that? What if, when people thought of you, they remembered you as a person who always stood up for others? What if you had a reputation for helping people who needed help? What if you were known as someone who cared about others more than you cared about yourself?

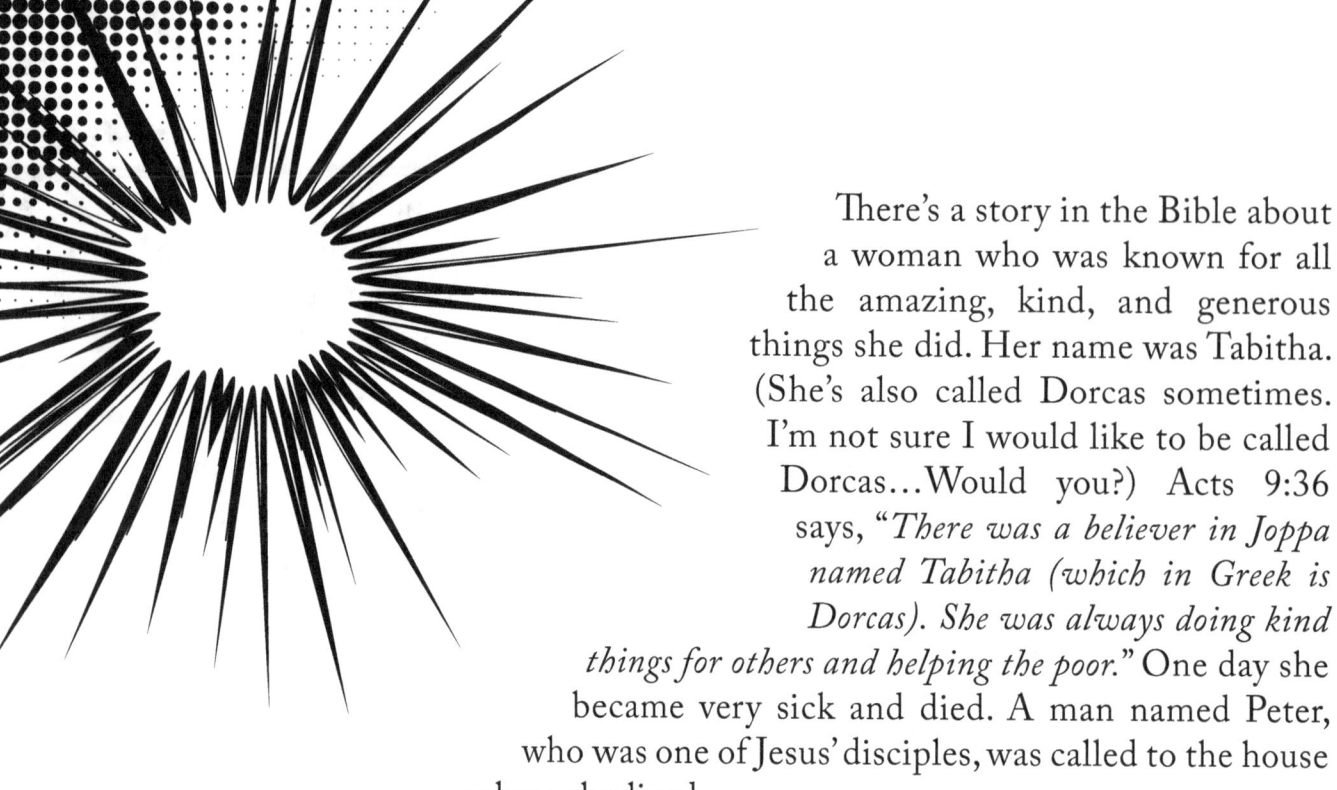

There's a story in the Bible about a woman who was known for all the amazing, kind, and generous things she did. Her name was Tabitha. (She's also called Dorcas sometimes. I'm not sure I would like to be called Dorcas...Would you?) Acts 9:36 says, *"There was a believer in Joppa named Tabitha (which in Greek is Dorcas). She was always doing kind things for others and helping the poor."* One day she became very sick and died. A man named Peter, who was one of Jesus' disciples, was called to the house where she lived.

"So Peter returned with them; and as soon as he arrived, they took him to the upstairs room. The room was filled with widows who were weeping and showing him the coats and other clothes Dorcas had made for them" (Acts 9:39). The house was full of people who knew and loved Tabitha because of the kind things she had done for them. It says that she had made them coats and sewed clothes for them. These were women whose husbands had died. They were probably very, very poor. Tabitha had taken it upon herself to take care of them, and that was what she was known for! (P.S. you should read the rest of the story in Acts 9 'cause something totally crazy incredible happens to Tabitha!)

BAZOOKA BOYS BONUS

The name Tabitha is a Hebrew name. Other times in the Bible, they call her by the name Dorcas, which is a Greek name. Both of the words mean "gazelle," which is an animal kind of like a deer. The Bible was originally written in these two languages, the Old Testament in Hebrew, and the New Testament in Greek! I'm thankful for the people who translated the Bible into English from these two languages so I can read it and understand it!

What I **LOVE** about this story is that Tabitha could have been known for a lot of other things, but she was known as someone who cared for other people. People loved her because she truly helped others. She wasn't always thinking about herself and how she could get attention for herself. **NO!** She thought of others first and how she could help them. That's the kind of attention I want!

We all love to get attention. But God wants us to be confident in Him, not needing to get so much attention from other people. When we know God loves us, we don't need to grab all the attention we can get from other people. We can feel strong and secure because we **KNOW** on the inside that we're important and matter to God.

Closing Prayer: *Dear God, I pray that You would help me to care for other people and not try and get attention in ways that aren't pleasing to you. Help me to be known for good things. I thank You that You love me and think I'm amazing! Amen.*

DOODLE PAGE

LESSON 7

Having people pay attention to us feels **GREAT!** But we have to be careful that we don't crave attention too much! On our superhero, make an imaginary list of all the things he's known for. (For example: maybe he flies super fast and can melt metal with his laser eyes!)

Now, draw a picture of yourself next to him. On the next page make a list of all the things **YOU** are known for. Be honest. Maybe you've made some mistakes and you've started to be known for some not-so-great things. Then, make a list of what you **WANT** to be known for!

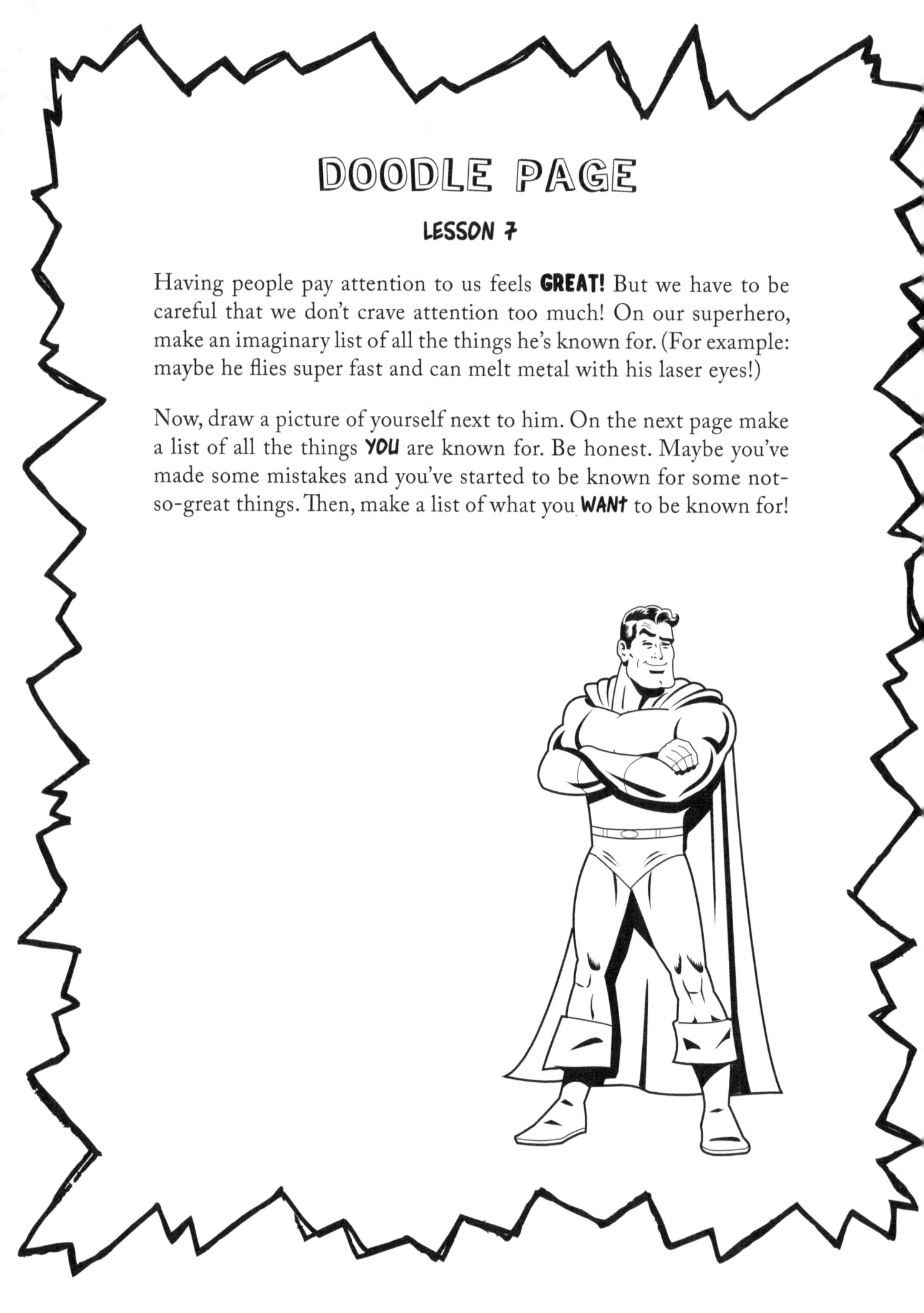

 # ACTIVITY SHEET

Tabitha was known as the woman who cared for other people. People loved her because she truly helped other people. She wasn't always thinking about herself and how she could get attention for herself.

Draw a picture of yourself helping someone!

Bazooka Boys ★ Relationships

God doesn't want us stealing all the attention! He doesn't want us to always make things about ourselves.

Fill in the missing letters in the verse below by substituting each number with the letter in the key to discover God's message.

    ___ ___n't be selfish; ___ ___n't try t___ impress ___thers.
     3 2   3 2   2   2

    Be humble, thinkin___ ___f ___thers as better than y___urselves.
                              1   2   2   2

—Philippians 2:3

KEY

G   O   D

1   2   3

Step 1: Read the amazing story of Tabitha in Act 9:36–43 in your NIV Bible and fill in the missing words.

36 In Joppa there was a disciple named _____ (which, when translated, is _____), she was always doing _____ and _____ the poor. 37 About that time she became sick and died, and her body was washed and placed in an _____ room. 38 _____ was near Joppa; so when the disciples heard that _____ was in Lydda, they sent two men to him and urged him, "Please come at once!"

39 Peter went with them, and when he arrived he was taken upstairs to the room. All the _____ stood around him, crying and showing him the _____ and other clothing that Dorcas had _____ while she was still with them.

⁴⁰ Peter sent them all out of the room; then he got down on his knees and _____. Turning toward the dead woman, he said, "Tabitha, get up." She _____ her eyes, and seeing Peter she sat up. ⁴¹ He took her by the _____ and helped her to her feet. Then he called for the _____ , especially the _____ and presented her to them _____. ⁴² This became known all over Joppa, and many people believed in the _____. ⁴³ Peter stayed in Joppa for some time with a tanner named Simon.

Step 2: Unscramble the missing words from the story of Tabitha

VELIA _____

SEELIREBV _____

ADCROS _____

DOGO _____

NDAH _____

LGPNEHI _____

DLOR _____

AYDLD _____

DMEA _____

Bazooka Boys ★ Relationships

EDPEON _____

REEPT _____

DPRYEA _____

WWOISD _____

ERBOS _____

AATTBIH _____

RAISPUTS _____

Step 3: Find the unscrambled missing words in the Word Search puzzle.

Word Search Puzzle

```
D W S E D S H U O U L D P B E
K E N A O N P W S N E R F O R
T H N E C S A R G O A D D Y L
O D T E T R E H H Y R I A N G
S W E A P V O D E O O A N M D
N O I T E O T D B R Y T O G E
T R A I T T E E N T P I O N F
S R L O M T S H E T H E I N G
S E V I L A W E W E A R T T R
B H E L P I N G Y I N A S E G
D O O G T O B E T H B E W C R
L E N T E R O F A I T T O E N
T O I O N O R D T O I N D G N
E G R A T I V H E T H I I N G
S V B D Z G A J U Y E Q W E J
```

Bazooka Boys ★ Relationships

BAZOOKA BREAKDOWN

God doesn't want us to steal all the attention. What are some ways in which we can try and get all the attention focused on us?

Absalom tried to get attention by doing a bunch of crazy things. Have you ever seen someone try and get attention by doing negative things? How did other people respond when they were doing bad things to try and get attention?

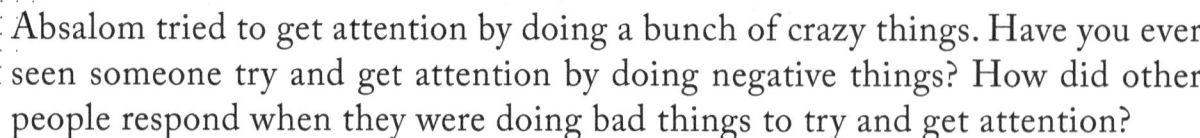

Bazooka Boys ★ Relationships

Draw a picture of yourself. Then write out some good things that you can be known for!

Write the theme verse three times and see if you can memorize it!

"We were not looking for praise from you or anyone else."
—1 Thessalonians 2:6 (NIRV)

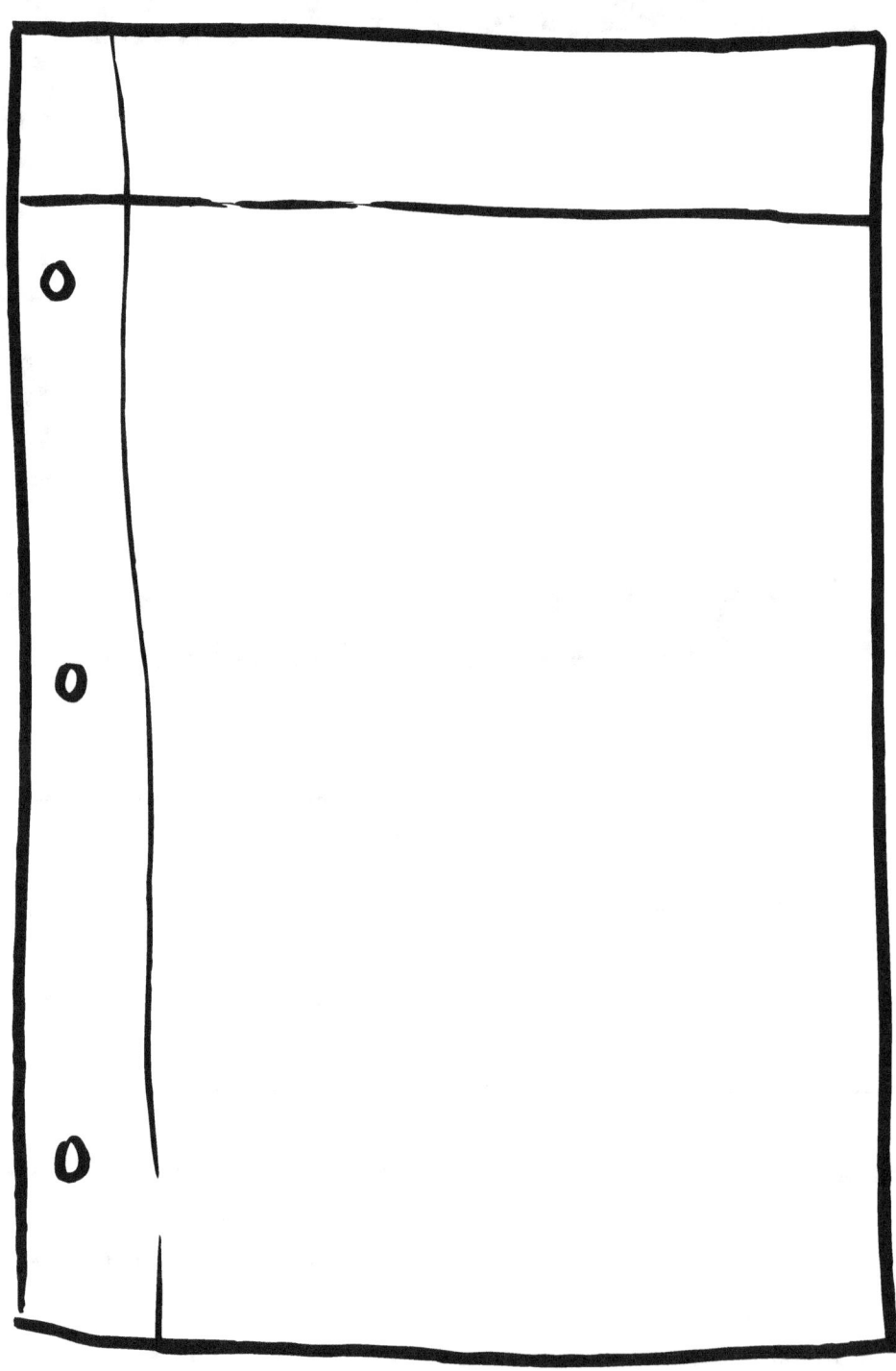

Bazooka Boys ★ Relationships

WEEK 7

RANDOM ACTS OF KINDNESS CARE KITS FOR THE HOMELESS

(20 minutes)

<u>Prep</u>

- Print the Random Acts of Kindness Care Kit supply list (*on page 133*).

<u>Supplies:</u>

- Kits
  - Soap
  - Lotion
  - Band Aids
  - Alcohol-free hand sanitizer
  - Alcohol-free mouthwash
  - Deodorant
  - Toothbrush
  - Toothpaste
  - Wet Ones wipes
  - Sunscreen
  - Granola bars
  - Bottled water
  - Most important—clean white athletic socks!
- White cardstock
- Markers

What Should We Do Next?

1. Place one of each item in a sock (including the other matching sock)

2. Someone who is homeless needs:

   - Clean socks are important because they don't have the luxury of throwing dirty socks into the wash each day.
   - Toothbrush, toothpaste, and mouthwash are important because most homeless don't get to go to the dentist.
   - Deodorant, soap, and wet wipes enable them to clean their bodies. They don't have access to regular showers and bathrooms.

3. Write a note of encouragement to put in their sock.

4. Keep in their car so they have it to bless someone in need.

RANDOM ACTS OF KINDNESS CARE KIT SUPPLY LIST:

- SOAP
- LOTION
- BAND AIDS
- ALCOHOL-FREE HAND SANITIZER
- ALCOHOL-FREE MOUTHWASH
- DEODORANT
- TOOTHBRUSH
- TOOTHPASTE
- WET ONES WIPES
- SUNSCREEN
- GRANOLA BARS
- BOTTLED WATER
- MOST IMPORTANT— CLEAN WHITE ATHLETIC SOCKS!

RANDOM ACTS OF KINDNESS CARE KIT SUPPLY LIST:

- SOAP
- LOTION
- BAND AIDS
- ALCOHOL-FREE HAND SANITIZER
- ALCOHOL-FREE MOUTHWASH
- DEODORANT
- TOOTHBRUSH
- TOOTHPASTE
- WET ONES WIPES
- SUNSCREEN
- GRANOLA BARS
- BOTTLED WATER
- MOST IMPORTANT— CLEAN WHITE ATHLETIC SOCKS!

MEAN PEOPLE

WHAT'S THE POINT?
Don't be a mean boy. And love the mean boys in your life.

THEME VERSE

*Love your enemies! Do good to those who hate you.
Bless those who curse you. Pray for those who hurt you.*
—Luke 6:27–28

RELATED BIBLE STORY

King David
Psalm 55

Sometimes people are mean.

And it really stinks.

Remember when we talked earlier about God's super secret weapon for dealing with relationships? What was the verse? *"Treat people in the same way that you want them to treat you."* (Luke 6:31, CEB)

Wouldn't it just be the most amazing thing in the world if everyone else treated **YOU** the way they want to be treated? If they only spoke kind words to you and never picked on you and never got mad at you? I think that would be ah-mazing.

But unfortunately, that's not the way things are. Even if you're nice and friendly, there will be moments when other people say mean things, treat you poorly, and generally make life stink.

Alexander had so much fun playing with the kids on his street…most of the time. Some days they could have the best time **EVER**, and then the next day

Bazooka Boys ★ Relationships

the boys would start picking on him and saying all kinds of mean things. He never really knew what to expect when he went to spend time with those "friends."

The **WORST** part was that he was starting to see himself behaving the same way. He got tired of always being the one picked on, so he started picking on other kids. It seemed like the only way to get them to stop was to make fun of someone else. But in his heart he knew that wasn't the way good friends treated one another.

So what should Alexander do? And what should we do in a situation where it seems like there's **LOTS** of fighting and picking on people? What does God want us to do?

Well, thankfully, God gives us some answers in the Bible to help us deal with all of these situations. I'm not saying that it will be easy, but doing the right thing rarely is.

First of all,

 **1. KEEP IT COOL.**

We have a saying at our house whenever anyone is going to play with their friends. We say, "Keep it cool." What in the world does that mean? Well, when you're with your friends, sometimes things can get tense pretty quick. Just like when Alexander was with his friends. One friend gets mad at the other friend and pretty soon someone is shoving or yelling or doing something stupid.

So, instead of letting things escalate quickly, what if you decided to just "keep it cool"? Instead of getting angry and reacting in a BIG way when your friend does something you don't like, instead of coming back quickly and full of anger, what if you just said, "Not cool, bro . . ." and then moved on? When someone starts to pick on someone (or YOU!) just look at them and say, "Not cool."

Proverbs 29:11 says, *"A foolish person lets his anger run wild. But a wise person keeps himself under control."* (NIRV) You can get angry and frustrated, but learn to talk about things with your friends and work them out calmly without all the drama. 'Cause you know what? The drama just makes everything worse.

Next time you're having a disagreement with your friend and you're tempted to start getting angry, tell yourself "keep it cool," and if they continue frustrating you or doing things that make you mad, stay calm and say "not cool."

(Oh yeah…and if your friend continues to be a jerk even when you're trying not to, don't give up. Just ignore it and move onto something else. It takes two people to have a fight, and if you don't dive into the mess, he'll eventually calm down too!)

The second thing we need to remember when dealing with mean people is

 ## 2. LOVE YOUR ENEMIES.

Corey was picked on by a boy at school **ALL THE TIME**. He made fun of his favorite backpack. He made fun of his school work. He made fun of his family. He shoved him at the bus stop. He made Corey's life **MISERABLE**.

Corey didn't know what to do. He talked to his dad about it, and they met with his teacher and the other boy and his parents. He was really embarrassed, but he knew that it was important to tell a grown up what was going on.

After the meeting, things got better, but something in Corey's heart got worse. She was **SO** angry at this boy. How could someone treat another person that way? Why did he do those things? Inside, he just wanted to get back at him. But he knew that God wanted him to forgive the person who had hurt him. He knew the Bible said, *"Love your enemies! Do good to those who hate you. Bless those who curse you. Pray for those who hurt you."* (Luke 6:27–28)

So, he asked God to help him love his enemy. He began to pray for the person who had hurt him. He showed kindness to him, even though he really wanted

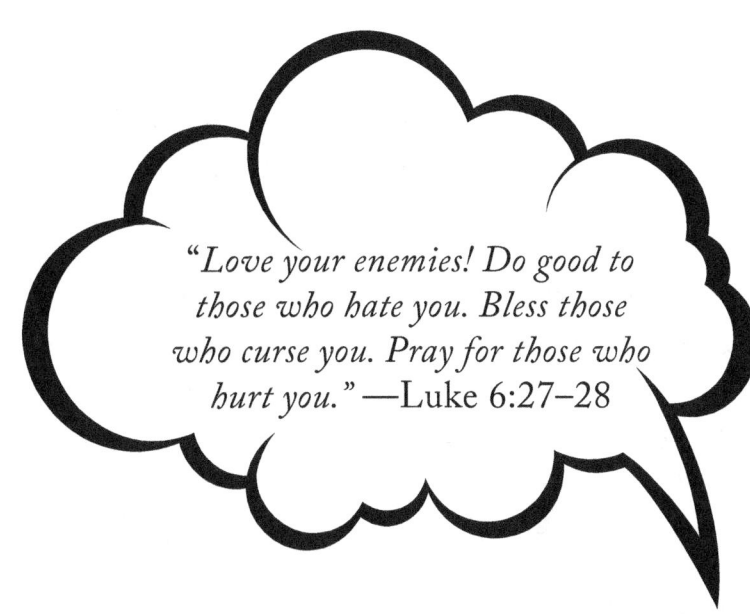

"Love your enemies! Do good to those who hate you. Bless those who curse you. Pray for those who hurt you." —Luke 6:27–28

to punch him in the face! And he didn't say bad things about him to other people.

Something amazing happened when Corey decided to do what the Bible said. He began to feel better. He didn't feel as angry anymore. Actually, God softened his heart so he could see that the boy was really just scared and insecure.

Now, it's not like he suddenly wanted to be his best friend! And he didn't start hanging out with him or anything like that. He didn't even really **LIKE** him. But God helped Corey love him by seeing him as one of God's sons…just like he was. He knew that God loved this boy, so he could love him, too, and even pray that he would get to know Jesus and that He would change his heart.

God will help you love your enemies.

But, what about another groups of people? What about people who USED to be your friends and now they won't be your friend anymore?

 ## 3. ASK GOD tO HELP YOU WITH BROKEN RELATIONSHIPS.

It's one thing to have a stranger pick on you and be mean to you, but it's a whole other thing when someone who **USED** to be a close friend suddenly won't be your friend anymore and starts being mean to you. This is one of the most painful things we can experience in our relationships. It's **REALLY** hard when our relationships are broken and someone who used to be our friend is now the person hurting us.

I think it hurts so much because they know so much about you. They were close to you and know what you're really like. It can be really hard because you can feel like you're not good enough. Like, someone got to know the real you, and once they got to know you, they just didn't want to be your friend anymore. That's **REALLY, REALLY** stinky!

This **EXACT** thing happened to someone in the Bible. King David writes about it in Psalm 55. He starts out by telling us that someone is **NOT** being very kind to him. He says, *"Listen to my prayer, O God. Do not ignore my cry for help! Please listen and answer me, for I am overwhelmed by my troubles. My enemies shout at me, making loud and wicked threats. They bring trouble on me and angrily hunt me down."* (Psalm 55:1–3) King David is NOT having a good day.

As we keep reading, we see who's giving him such a hard time. *"This isn't the neighborhood bully mocking me—I could take that. This isn't a foreign devil spitting invective—I could tune that out. It's you! We grew up together! You! My best friend! Those long hours of leisure as we walked arm in arm, God a third party to our conversation."* (Psalm 55:12–14, MSG)

It's someone who used to be his friend—his best friend! Can you imagine how sad King David must have felt? The person causing him so much trouble was actually someone who was supposed to be a friend.

If you have a person who used to be your friend who is now being mean to you, I am really, really sorry. I know that's very hard, and I'm sorry this has happened to you. But, you can do exactly what King David did! He asked God to help him. Psalm 55: 16 says, *"But I will call on God, and the Lord will rescue me."* Ask God to help you know what to do in the situation. Maybe you need to apologize for something. Maybe you need to reach out to them in kindness. Or maybe you just need to let it go and ask God to help you forgive the person who has hurt you.

BOOM!

Man, it's **SO** hard to forgive the people who hurt us. It's hard to let go when everything in us wants to fight back and make them hurt the way we're hurting. But God wants you to forgive others. Colossians 3:13

Bazooka Boys ★ Relationships

says, *"Make allowance for each other's faults, and forgive anyone who offends you. Remember, the Lord forgave you, so you must forgive others."*

Ask God to help you let go of your hurt and anger. Ask Him to help you forgive.

So, what if you and I decided we were going to just **STOP** all the mean stuff? What if we just said, "You know what, I will just choose to be a kind person." If we chose to forgive and love those who hurt us, and yet always show love and stick up for the boys who are being hurt by other people, we could really change a lot of things.

SO LET'S DO IT! NO MORE MEAN.

During your project time tonight, you're going to sign the **Bazooka Boys NO MORE MEAN Treaty**. It says this:

> "I promise, as Bazooka Boy and as a son of God, to treat other kids with kindness and respect. I will not be mean. I will keep it cool. And I will forgive and love those who are mean to me instead of being mean back. I will show the love of Jesus in the way I talk, act, and treat my friends."

Closing Prayer: *Dear God, I thank You for promising to always be with me no matter what I'm going through. Help me know what to do when other kids are being mean to me. Help me "keep it cool" and forgive and love those who are mean to me. I promise that I will be kind and loving to the people around me, because it will make You happy. I love You. Amen.*

ACTIVITY SHEET

What should you do when you're in a situation where it seems like there's **LotS** of tension and fighting and maybe even someone picking on you for no reason? The following verses tell us how to treat people who hurt us.

Step 1: Find the hidden words from the list in the Word Search puzzle.

Step 2: Place the hidden words in the correct blank in the Bible verse.

Step 3: Go to your Bible and find Luke 6:27–28 (NLT) to check your answer.

"_____ your enemies! Do _____ to those who hate you. _____ those who curse you. _____ for those who hurt you" (Luke 6:27–28, NLT).

WORD SEARCH PUZZLE

```
N  O  O  T  B  B
V  T  A  F  M  L
P  E  E  G  U  E
R  S  F  O  V  S
A  F  S  O  X  S
Y  D  L  D  M  T
```

WORD LIST:
Bless   Love   Good   Pray

Jesus died on the cross so that the sins of all people could be forgiven. He did this out of love.

Solve the puzzle to find out what God wants us to do for the people who have hurt us.

Bazooka Boys ★ Relationships

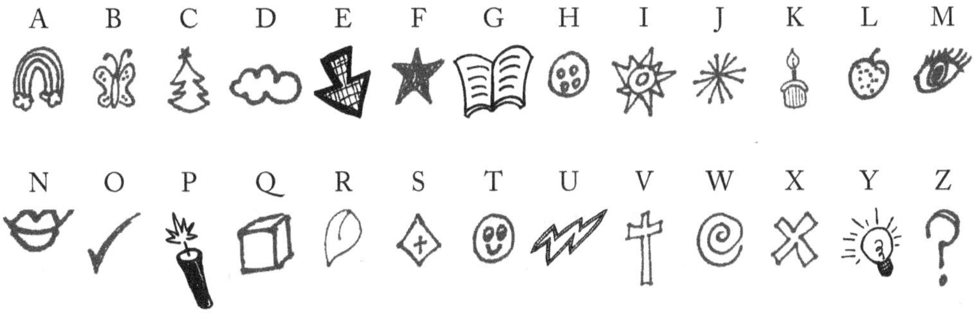

A	B	C	D	E	F	G	H	I	J	K	L	M
🌈	🦋	🎄	☁	⬇	★	📖	😮	✴	✳	🕯	🍓	👁

N	O	P	Q	R	S	T	U	V	W	X	Y	Z
👄	✓	🧨	⬜	🍃	◇	🙂	⚡	✝	🌀	✖	💡	?

Luke

 !

Answer: *Love your enemies! Do good to those who curse you. Bless those who curse you. Pray for those who curse you. Pray for those who hurt you.* Luke 6:26-27

6:26-27 NLT

145

Look up the Bible passages below and fill in the blank lines with the missing letters.

When you have filled in all the blank lines, put the circled letters in the matching numbered lines to find out what God wants us to do for the people who have hurt us. All scripture NIV.

A fool gives full ___ ___ ___ ___ *to bring calm in their rage, but the wise*
                      3   15
bring calm in the end. – Proverbs 29:11

Do to ___ ___ ___ ___ ___ ___ *as you would have them do to you.* – Luke 6:31
       2

As for me, I ___ ___ ___ ___ *to God, and the* ___ ___ ___ ___ *saves me.*
                     1   7
– Psalm 55:16

Bear with each other and ___ ___ ___ ___ ___ ___ ___ *one another*
                                  12 13   4,17
if any of you has a grievance against someone. Forgive as the Lord forgave you.
– Colossians 3:13

And when you stand ___ ___ ___ ___ ___ ___ ___ *, if you hold*
                          8   5,10   6
anything against anyone, forgive him, so that your Father in heaven may forgive your sins. – Mark 11:25

Then Peter came to Jesus and asked, "Lord, how many times shall I forgive
___ ___   ___ ___ ___ ___ ___ ___ *or sister who sins against me?*
18   9,14   16

Jesus answered, "I tell ___ ___ ___ *, not seven times, but seventy-seven times.*
                            11
—Matthew 18:21-22

Bazooka Boys ★ Relationships

WEEK 8

Word List

you　　　　*others*　　　　*praying*　　　　*call*
vent　　　　*brother*　　　　*forgive*　　　　*my*
Lord

God's instruction is to:

___ ___ ___ ___   ___ ___ ___   ___ ___ ___ ___
 1   2   3   4   5   6   7   8   9 10 11

___ ___ ___   ___ ___ ___ ___.
12 13 14   15 16 17 18

Bazooka Boys ★ Relationships

BAZOOKA BREAKDOWN

When someone has been mean to you, what are some things you **WANT** to do to get back at them. Write them out in the circles.

Now, think of some things that you should do **INSTEAD** of being mean. Cross out the mean things and write in the right way to handle yourself.

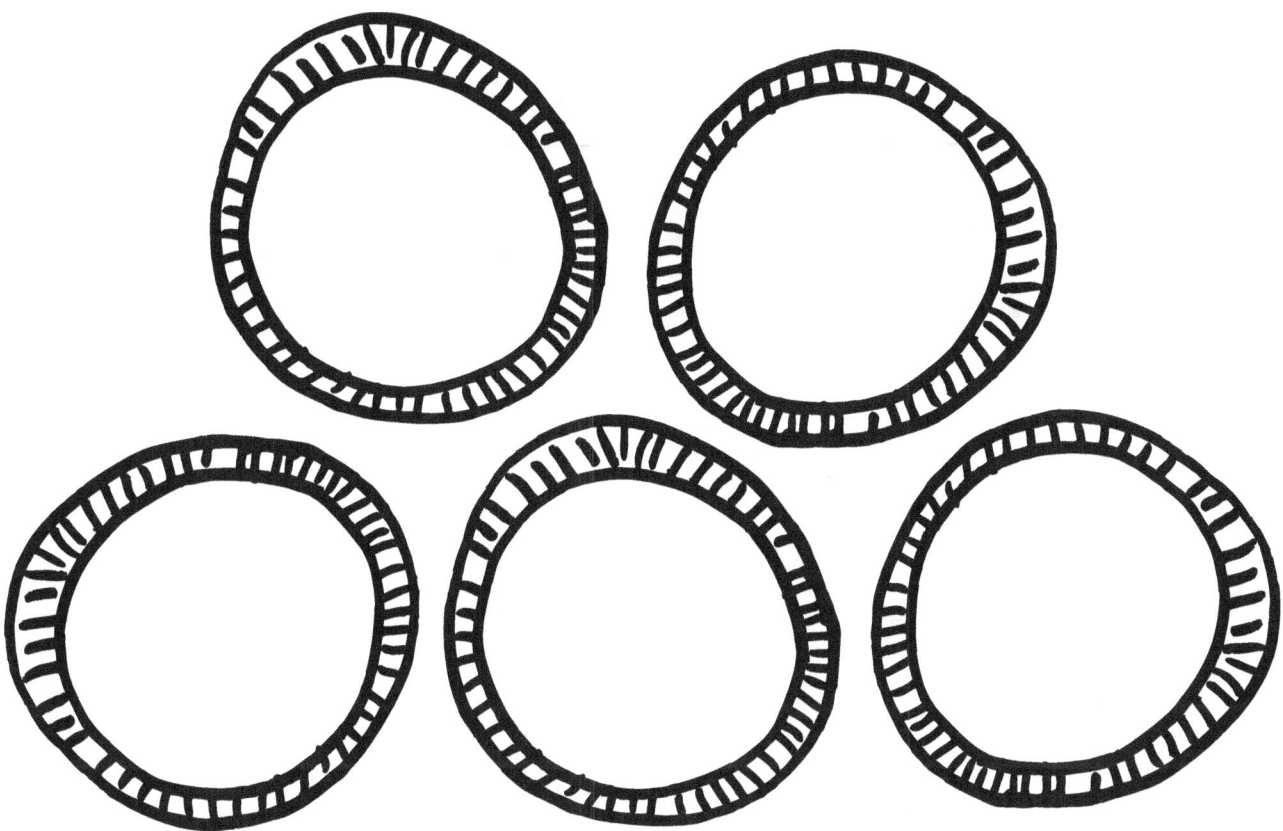

We learned that when we are in a situation where feelings are starting to escalate and people are getting angry, that we should remind ourselves to **KEEP IT COOL**. Color in the words below.

KEEP IT COOL

God says that we are to love our enemies. Think of someone who has hurt you or been mean to you. In the space provided write out a prayer for them. Ask God to help you see them the way that He sees them.

DEAR GOD, I PRAY FOR

_____.

_____

_____

_____

_____

_____

_____

_____

_____

_____.

Write out the theme verse three times and see if you can memorize it!

*"Love your enemies! Do good to those who hate you.
Bless those who curse you.
Pray for those who hurt you."*
—Luke 6:27-28

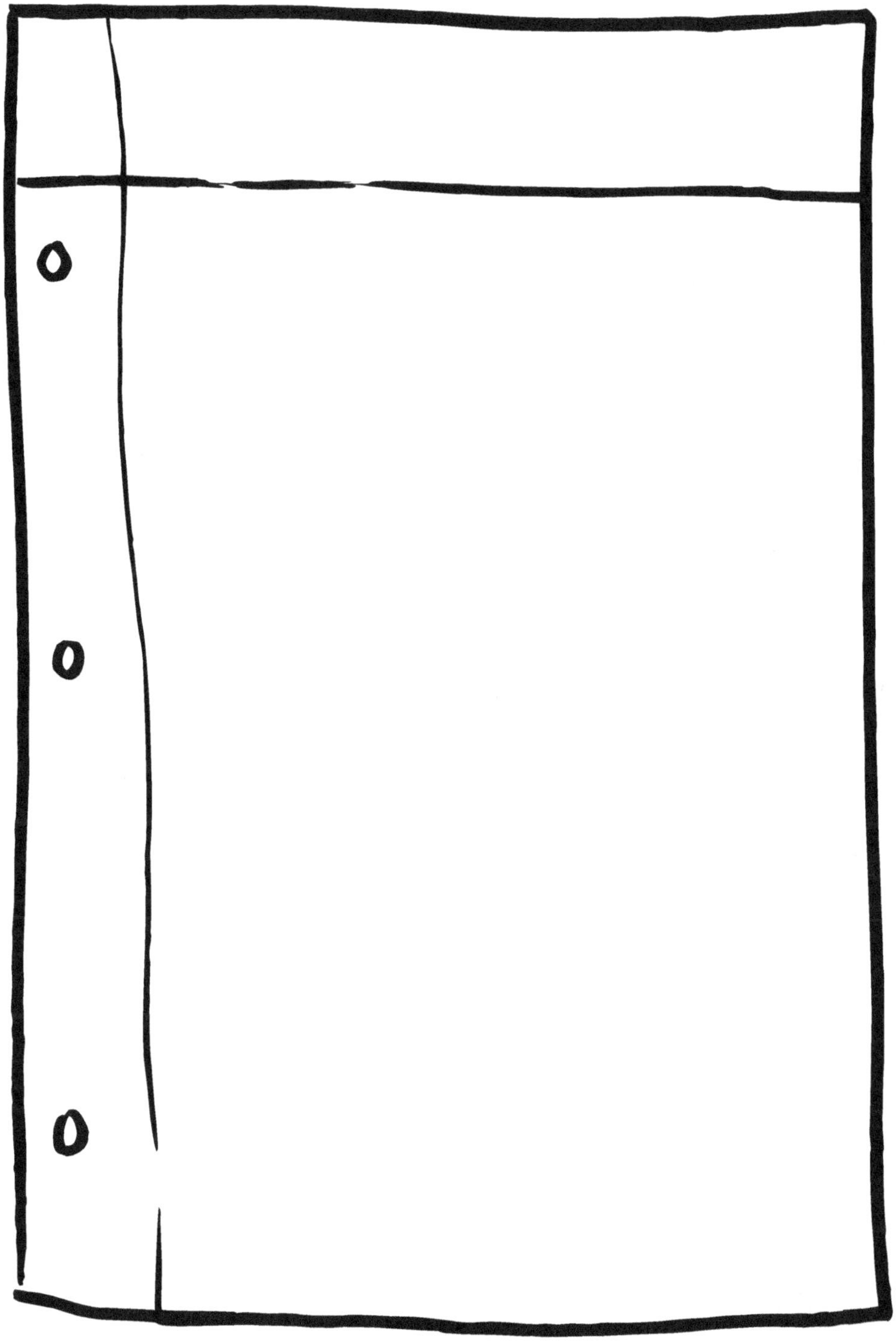

NO MORE MEAN TREATY

(20 minutes)

Supplies:

- No More Mean Treaty template
- White cardstock
- Various patterns and colors of scrapbook paper
- Black poster board
- Crayons/markers

Prep

1. Copy No More Mean Treaty Template onto white cardstock.

What Should We Do Next?

1. Color the No More Mean Treaty.

2. Sign the No More Mean Treaty.

3. Mount scrapbook paper onto black poster board with Elmer's glue.

4. Hang the signed treaty in your room to remind yourself to follow the Bazooka Boys No Mean Treaty!

I promise, as **BAZOOKA BOY**
and as a son of God,
to treat others with kindness
and respect.

I will keep it cool.

I will not be mean.

And I will forgive and love
those who are mean to me,
instead of being mean back.

I will show the love of Jesus
in the way I talk, act,
and treat my friends.

Signed by: _____

Date: _____

DO THE RIGHT THING

WHAT'S THE POINT?
God wants you to stand up for what's right.

THEME VERSE

Do what is right. Then you will be accepted. If you don't do what is right, sin is waiting at your door to grab you. It longs to have you. But you must rule over it.
—Genesis 4:7 (NIRV)

RELATED BIBLE STORY

King Josiah
2 Kings 22

This entire series has been about how important our relationships are. God has blessed us with incredible friends and family who walk through our lives with us. They remind us that we're not alone and they can help us become the very best we can be!

But sometimes our relationships can become so important to us that we're willing to do anything to make the people in our lives happy.

Austin loved hanging out with his friends. One day, he was at the store with his friend Spencer. Suddenly, he saw Spencer take a piece of candy from the shelf and put it in his pocket without paying for it. Austin couldn't believe it! Then it got worse. Spencer took another piece of candy and put it in Austin's pocket, too. Austin didn't know what to do. He knew that it was wrong to steal, but he didn't want his friend to get mad at him. He didn't say anything and then spent the rest of the day feeling like he was going to puke.

Sometimes our friends try to get us to do things we know we shouldn't do. Sometimes our friends say things we know aren't pleasing to God. And sometimes our friends can behave in a way we **KNOW** isn't right.

What should we do in those moments? Does a good friend just overlook those things and not say anything? Or does a good friend stand up for what's right?

The answer is **ALWAYS** that a good friend stands up for what's right. A good friend wants their friends to make right choices. Sometimes that means you have to speak up when your friends are doing something wrong. And even if that means your friend gets mad at you or **EVEN** says they won't be your friend anymore, it's better for you to do what's right.

Bazooka Boys ★ Relationships

BAZOOKA BOYS BONUS

If someone tells you they aren't going to be your friend anymore unless you do what they tell you—even if it's something you don't want to do or something you know is wrong—that person isn't a very good friend. GOOD friends don't make other people do things they know are wrong. And good friends always help you make good choices, not bad ones. Make sure you surround yourself with good friends!

This can be **REALLY** hard! Reeeeeealllllyyy hard. No one likes to have their friends mad at them. It's not easy to speak up when everyone else is just going along with what's happening. It's very hard to stand up and do what's right when everyone else is doing what's wrong.

But God always wants you to do the right thing. He asks us to stand up and speak up. 1 Peter 3:14 says, *"But even if you suffer for doing what is right, God will reward you for it. So don't worry or be afraid of their threats."* Even when we're scared of what our friends might say, we need to honor God by doing what's right.

How do we do this? How can we get the courage to do the right thing even when we feel **HUGE** pressure to just go along with what everyone else is doing?

First of all, we need to

 **1. LIVE tO PLEASE GOD.**

Austin really liked his friend Spencer. He always sat with him at lunch and walked home from school with him. He hated the idea of Spencer being mad at him and she couldn't imagine what it would be like if he wouldn't be his friend anymore.

But in his heart, he knew what Spencer was doing was wrong. He knew he shouldn't take things he hadn't paid for and that it wouldn't please his parents and, especially, wouldn't please God.

The problem was that Austin was more worried about what his **FRIEND** would think than what **GOD** would think. He was more worried about making his **FRIEND** happy than making **GOD** happy. Proverbs 29:25 says, *"Fearing people is a dangerous trap, but to trust in the Lord means safety."*

What would have given Austin the courage to do the right thing? He should have been more worried about pleasing **GOD** than pleasing his friend.

We **HAVE** to care more about what God thinks than **ANYONE ELSE**. We have to do the things that will make **HIM** happy even if it means our friends might be upset with us. Choosing the right thing always pleases God. And we have to live to please God instead of pleasing other people.

> "FEARING PEOPLE IS A DANGEROUS TRAP, BUT TO TRUST IN THE LORD MEANS SAFETY."
> —Proverbs 29:25

When we fail to stand up for what's right, we're usually more concerned about pleasing our friends than we are about pleasing God. John 12:43 talks about some people who were having this **EXACT** problem. It says, *"For they loved human praise more than the praise of God."* People were making wrong choices because they wanted to make people happy **MORE** than they wanted to make God happy.

Make the decision today that you're **ALWAYS** going to do the thing that will please God. Make **HIM** first in your life, and in the moments when you're feeling scared to stand up to your friends, you'll **KNOW** in your heart that you **HAVE** to please God more than other people.

The second way we can stand up for what is right is to,

 ## 2. KNOW WHAT THE BIBLE SAYS, AND THEN DO IT!

There's a story in the Bible about a young man named Josiah. Josiah became the King of Judah when he was eight years old! Can you imagine? In the years before Josiah became King, the other leaders of Judah had decided to walk away from God. They didn't do all the things the Bible told them to do anymore. Actually, Josiah didn't even **KNOW** about the law and the commands of God! His parent's hadn't taught Him about the things God said were right and wrong.

But Josiah had a heart that wanted to please God. One day, his high priest discovered the scrolls in the Temple that had the laws of God written on them. The high priest told Josiah what the law said, and Josiah became very upset because he realized that all the people were not doing the things God had asked them to do. He said this to the high priest, *"Go to the Temple and speak to the Lord for me and for the people and for all Judah. Inquire about the words written in this scroll that has been found. For the Lord's great anger is burning against us because our ancestors have not obeyed the words in this scroll. We have not been doing everything it says we must do."* (2 Kings 22:13)

Just So You Know

The scrolls Josiah discovered were the special laws that God had given Moses. They were all the rules from God about the way He wanted us to live. Those laws are now a part of the Bible we have today. Most of them can be found in the book of Deuteronomy!

Once Josiah understood the way God wanted him and all the people of Judah to live, he went to work. He tore down all the idols in the land because the law told him to. He had the people say they were sorry for their behavior because the scrolls told him to. He made all the changes the law told him to make because he wanted to honor God. 2 Kings 22:2 says this about Josiah: *"He did what was pleasing in the Lord's sight and followed the example of his ancestor David. He did not turn away from doing what was right."*

If you're going to do the things God wants you to do, you need to know the Bible! Josiah wasn't doing the things that God wanted just because He didn't know any better! You need to read your Bible and learn what God says we should do. And we should also read the Bible to learn the things that God says we shouldn't do!

The Bible is so **AMAZING**. It can give us wisdom and insight in SO many areas of our lives. It can help us know how to be a kind friend, a good son, a hard worker, and many, many other things. 2 Timothy 3:16 says, *"All Scripture is inspired by God and is useful to teach us what is true and to make us realize what is wrong in our lives. It corrects us when we are wrong and teaches us to do what is right."*

God will show you the right way to live your life through the words He wrote to you in the Bible. **BUT** you have to read it and learn what it says! That's why it's so important to read your Bible every day—so you can know the things God wants you to do!

And the last way you can do the right thing is to

 ## 3. BE A LEADER.

When Josiah discovered the law, he quickly changed the things in his own life that weren't pleasing to God. But he did even more than that! He led the other people in his nation back to the ways of God.

God wants you to make the right choices and He wants you to help **LEAD** other people into the right choices as well. There will come a moment sometime in your life when a group of friends is heading for a wrong choice. Maybe your friends are looking at pictures or videos they shouldn't be looking at or picking on someone who is weaker than them. In those moments, you have a choice. You can go along with what everyone else is doing, or you can stand up and be a leader! Instead of following other people down the wrong path, you can stand up and lead your friends down the **RIGHT** path!

God doesn't want you to follow other people. He wants you to be a leader! He doesn't want you to do whatever other people say, even when you know it's wrong. He wants you to lead your friends into doing the right thing!

There's a verse in Deuteronomy about being a leader. It says, *"If you listen to these commands of the Lord your God that I am giving you today, and if you carefully obey them, the Lord will make you the head and not the tail, and you will always be on top and never at the bottom."* (Deuteronomy 28:13)

Bazooka Boys ★ Relationships

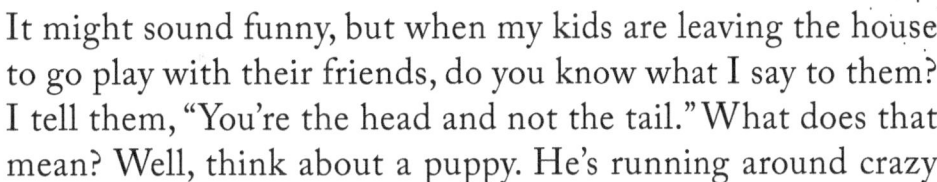

It might sound funny, but when my kids are leaving the house to go play with their friends, do you know what I say to them? I tell them, "You're the head and not the tail." What does that mean? Well, think about a puppy. He's running around crazy and wild and wagging his tail. What is deciding where that puppy is going to go: his head or his tail? His **HEAD**! The head is the leader of the dog. The tail just follows behind.

You and I are the head and not the tail! We should be leading our friends into **GOOD** things, not following our friends into bad things. We should not follow our friends into doing things we know will not please God. We should lead our friends into things that we know are right! **YOU** are the head and not the tail. You are a leader, not a follower. And you can choose the **RIGHT** thing instead of following people into the wrong thing!

God wants you to stand up for what's right. Genesis 4:7 says, *"Do what is right. Then you will be accepted. If you don't do what is right, sin is waiting at your door to grab you. It longs to have you. But you must rule over it."* (NIRV) You have a choice. You can do the right thing, or you can choose the wrong thing. God is there to help you make the right choices and live a life that honors Him.

Closing Prayer: *Dear God, I want to stand up for the right thing. Help me to want to please You more than I want to please my friends. I will read your Word and do the things it tells me to do. I want to be a leader who shows other people how to honor You. Amen.*

DOODLE PAGE

LESSON 9

The Bible says we're to be leaders, not followers. We should be in the front, making good decisions, not in the back just following what everyone else is doing.

On the train, draw a picture of yourself in the car you want to be on! Then, in the space provided, write "**I AM A LEADER!**" in big letters and color the rest of the train.

ACTIVITY SHEET

WEEK 9

Deuteronomy 28:13 NLT talks about being a leader. It says, *"If you listen to these commands of the Lord your God that I am giving you today, and if you carefully obey them, the Lord will make you the* **HEAD** *and* **NOT** *the* **TAIL**, *and you will always be on top and never at the bottom."*

Color the puppy below and remember that it's his head that decides where he wants to go and what he wants to do. The head is the leader of the dog. His tail just follows behind.

Read the verses below and fill in the blanks below with the word **RIGHT**.

Do what is _____. Then you will be accepted. If you don't do what is right, sin is waiting at your door to grab you. It longs to have you. But you must rule over it. – Genesis 4:7 NIRV

But even if you suffer for doing what is _____, God will reward you for it. So don't worry or be afraid of their threats. –1 Peter 3:14 NLT

He did what was pleasing in the Lord's sight and followed the example of his ancestor David. He did not turn away from doing what was _____.
– 2 Kings 22:2 NLT

All Scripture is inspired by God and is useful to teach us what is true and to make us realize what is wrong in our lives. It corrects us when we are wrong and teaches us to do what is _____. – 2 Timothy 3:16 NLT

Unscramble the words below, place them in the correct part of the scripture verse and discover what God has to say about leadership!

Step 1 – Unscramble the words

dhae   ____ ____ ____ ____

ltia   ____ ____ ____ ____

mmcadsno   ____ ____ ____ ____ ____ ____ ____ ____

Bazooka Boys ★ Relationships

dLro   ___ ___ ___ ___

wflloo   ___ ___ ___ ___ ___ ___

tbtomo   ___ ___ ___ ___ ___ ___

Step 2 – Fill in the blanks of the scripture verse below with the correct unscrambled word from step one.

The **LORD** will make you the ___ ___ ___ ___,

not the ___ ___ ___ ___.

If you pay attention to the ___ ___ ___ ___ ___ ___ ___ ___

of the ___ ___ ___ ___ your God that I give you this day and carefully

___ ___ ___ ___ ___ ___ them, you will always be at the top, never

at the ___ ___ ___ ___ ___ ___.

Step 3 – Check your answer by reading Deuteronomy 28:13 NIV.

Word List

Lord   *tail*   *bottom*   *commands*   *follow*   *head*

God wants you to ____ ____ ____ ____ ____ ____ ____!

Step 1 - Read each verse below and fill in the blank. (All scripture NIV)

"But even if you should _____ for what is right, you are blessed. Do not fear what they fear; do not be frightened." —1 Peter 3:14

"Fear of man will prove to be a snare, but whoever _____ in the LORD is kept safe." —Proverbs 29:25

"If you do what is right, will you not be _____? But if you do not do what is right, sin is crouching at your door; it desires to have you, but you must master it." —Genesis 4:7

"Am I now trying to win the approval of human beings, or of God? Or am I trying to please people? If I were still trying to please people, I would _____ be a servant of Christ." —Galations 1:10

"He did what was right in the eyes of the LORD and followed completely the ways of his father _____, not turning aside to the right or to the left." —2 Kings 22:2

"All Scripture is God-breathed and is _____ for teaching, rebuking, correcting and training in righteousness." —2 Timothy 3:16

"...for they loved _____ praise more than praise from God." —John 12:43

Bazooka Boys ★ Relationships

Step 2 – Circle the first letter of each missing word from the previous page, and put that letter into the blank spaces below to find out what God wants you to do!

Word List

David   *not*   *useful*   *accepted*
suffer   *trusts*

BAZOOKA BREAKDOWN

It can be scary to stand up to our friends when they want us to do something that isn't right. Imagine what this boy might be thinking if his friends were wanting him to do something wrong. Write out his thoughts in the text bubbles below.

Bazooka Boys ★ Relationships

King Josiah learned what the Bible said and then worked hard to follow the things it told him to do. Is there something you have worked hard to do (or stop doing) because the Bible told you to?

Write out the theme verse three times and see if you can memorize it!

"Do what is right. Then you will be accepted. If you don't do what is right, sin is waiting at your door to grab you. It longs to have you. But you must rule over it."
—Genesis 4:7 NIRV

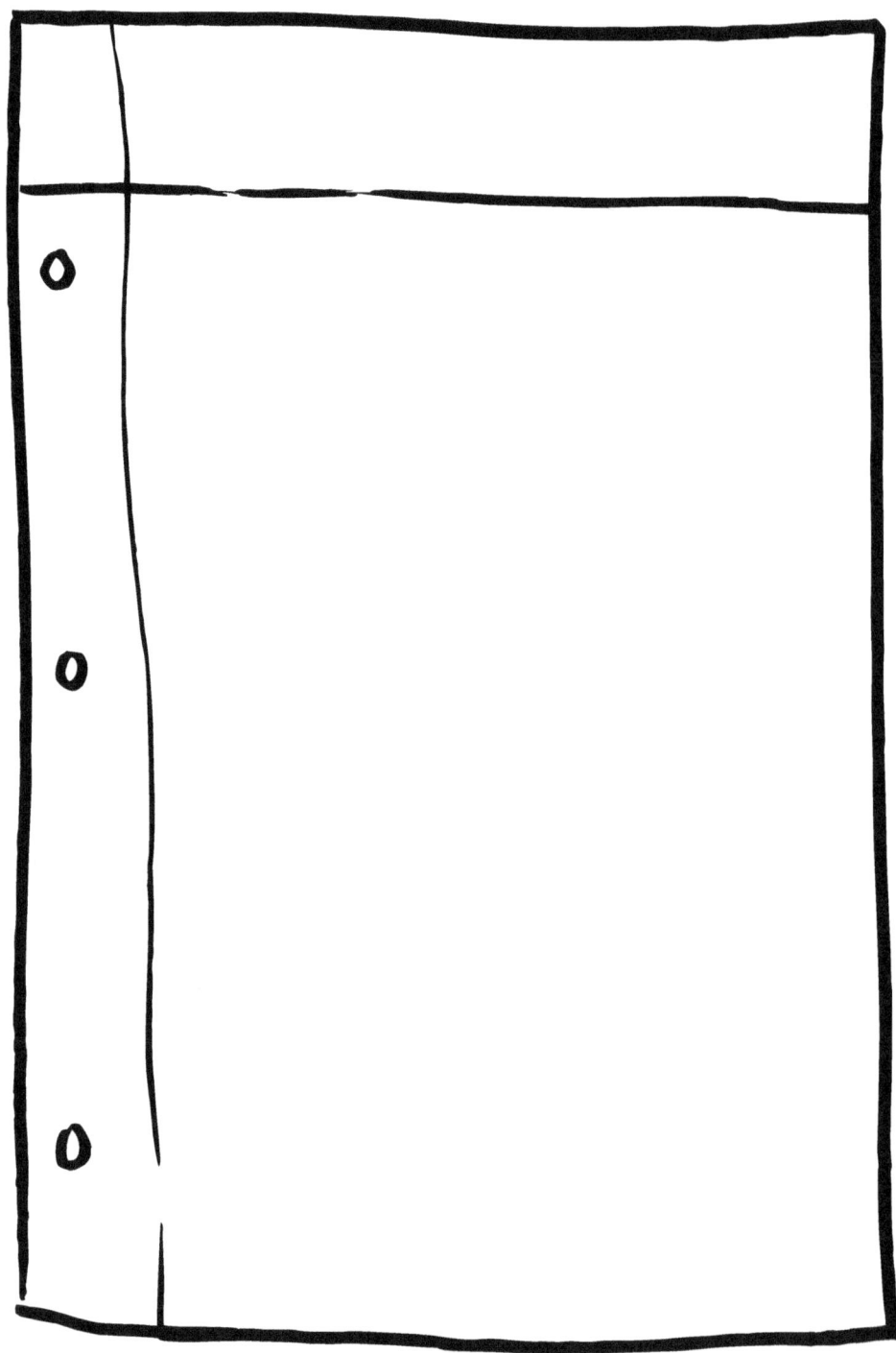

Bazooka Boys ★ Relationships

BE THE HEAD NOT THE TAIL CROSS

Supplies Needed:

- Wood cross (one cross) (Michaels/Hobby Lobby/JoAnn Fabrics)
- Copper or metallic paint (optional)
- Paint Brush (optional)
- Blow dryer (optional) - the blow dryer will quicken the drying time
- Pennies (a lot of pennies)
- Wood or Tacky Glue

What Should We Do Next?

1. Paint the wood cross with the metallic paint (optional)

2. Blow dry or let cross dry naturally (optional)

3. Glue pennies HEAD side up on the cross in a pattern

This cross is a reminder to obey God's word and to be a good leader by being the head and not the tail.